# Lead The Stampede


# By Marc Guberti

**A Note To The Reader**

Wherever you are in your niche, this book will provide you with the recipe needed to become an established leader in that niche. There are plenty of reasons why people want to become leaders in their niche. The leaders get more visibility, more business opportunities, and earn more revenue. The leaders of a particular niche are the go-to experts for the answers. The leaders are the people who the masses look up to. The leaders are significant people in their niches who will be missed when they are gone.

Many people think that leadership is something that comes naturally. In other words, either you have the talent or you don't. On the contrary, leadership, just like anything else in life, can be learned by anyone at any time. There are characteristics that make up every leader that I will discuss in these pages. In addition to sharing these characteristics with you, I will show you how to make these characteristics a part of your life so you can be a leader in your niche. Throughout this book will be examples of people utilizing these characteristics into their products, services, and expertise.

# Table Of Contents

# What Is The Stampede?

There are millions of niches to choose from. There's the social media expert niche, the real estate niche, the sports niche, the dog training niche, the food niche, and many others. No matter what niche you choose, there is going to be competition. Some niches have millions of competitors while other niches have thousands of competitors. There are people who seek to escape the competition, but the competition follows every move. Henry Ford's Model T truly revolutionized the entire car industry. He escaped the competition, but in this day and age, car companies have caught up. There are now numerous companies competing with Ford such as Toyota, Tesla Motors, Mercedes Benz, and others as well. Creating a new niche will give you a big lead, but competitors will do everything in their power to become a part of the new niche and catch up to you. This is when a stampede develops, the rush to become the leader of an emerging or long-established industry.

**Envision Your Niche As A Stampede**
Everyone in your competition strives to become the best person or business in their niche. There is the best person as well as other people and businesses that are not too far behind. There are millions of customers who buy products from you and your competitors. Most of these customers go to the people who are leading their respective stampedes. They go to the best service, the popular name, and the best product in the marketplace.

Competitors are doing everything they can to get further ahead of everyone else. Some competitors slash their *prices*. If the average training course costs $100, some of the competitors will slash their prices and only charge $50 for a training course. If the average piece of furniture costs $550, some of the competitors will slash their prices and only charge $450 for their pieces of furniture. If the average video game costs $50, some of the competitors will slash their prices and only charge $40 for their video games. Other competitors decide that high *quality* is the way to go. If the average training course offers 2 hours of content, some of the competitors will decide to offer 6 hours worth of video content. If the average iPhone app has 5 functions, some of the competitors will decide to create iPhone apps with 10 functions. If the average computer takes 1 second to load the internet, some of the competitors will decide to create a computer that loads the internet in milliseconds. Some competitors also have a strong belief that *convenience* is everything. They get the best customer support team that responds to all questions within 24 hours with the right answers. We have all had the moment when we had a question, and since no one could answer it, we had to spend countless hours looking for the answer on Google. Having a powerful customer service team eliminates that problem for some businesses.

It does not take long for a successful method that someone started to then be modified and implemented by others. Case studies start to develop. There are stories about how one person made millions of dollars by following some unconventional methods. The guy who sold his video game for $40 ends up getting 1 million sales every month. The guy whose iPhone app has 10 different functions ends up getting 10 times as many sales as the average iPhone app. The person with the 6 hour training course for $50 goes viral. At some point, the sales for these types of products flood in.

After hearing about the success stories, competitors want the same success and fortune that the few of their niche have. Many competitors research how the successful person achieved the success and fortune. The competition will then try to duplicate the methods that the successful person used. The problem is that too many people will try to duplicate the methods. The low prices will become normal. $2.99 Kindle eBooks used to be rare, but now they are easy to find. Competitors will either have to lower their prices even more, or find another way to lead their own stampede.

In order to grow, you need to search for methods that people are not using already. If you find a method of growth before anyone else, you will catapult closer to the front of the stampede. The best part is that you get established as the main person who used the method. After hearing about the person who sold video games for $40, other people try to copy the $40 method, but the first person to use this method is already established as the main person. Everyone notices the first person's video games being worth $40. The next few people get attention as well. However, there are more video games that are suddenly worth $40. Many people want to use the method, but as more people use the method, less of the newcomers benefit from it. The early bird gets the worm, but most people end up being the late birds.

## The Solution Is Not Just A Lower Price Tag

A lower price alone does not stand a chance. Selling a Kindle eBook for $0.99 or a video game for $30 is not going to be enough. The competition will just catch up and reduce their prices to match yours. When they do that, some of your competitors will focus on providing a little more value than you for the same price.

Offering your product or service for a lower price is one piece of the puzzle. The other piece of the puzzle is creating something that makes you stand out to a different group of people. A lower price tag combined with something completely different from the competition that provides value will give you a big edge and the leading position of your niche's stampede.

## Why Lead The Stampede?

No matter which niche you settle in, competitors will be in your niche trying to lead the stampede. Leading the stampede will result in more people seeing you which also means more sales, more business opportunities, and more connections. In a marathon race, all of the spectators can clearly see the first few runners. Then, the thousands of other people come in, and remembering all of those people is nearly impossible. Being the leader of the stampede allows you to run off where the thousands of other runners can't catch you.

The journey from the back of the stampede to the front of the stampede is a journey like no other. However, when you are at the front of the stampede as the competition struggles to keep up, you will be glad that you went on the journey. By leading the stampede, you will become the go-to expert for your niche. If you lead the stampede for the social media expert niche, people will go to you. People will be sending you emails asking you for consultation or to speak at a public event. When you lead the stampede, you get noticed far more than the people who are stuck in the middle or the back of the stampede.

**12 Characteristics Needed To Lead The Stampede**

Neither success nor failure are final. It is possible for a late bird to go from the back of the stampede to the front. It is possible for someone in the front of the stampede to drop back. The reason people move forward or back is because of the 12 characteristics addressed below. In the upcoming chapters, I will go into further detail about each of these characteristics. Here's what they are and what you need to know about them for now:

1. **Good Planning**: In order to get your goals accomplished and become successful, you need to have an effective plan. Not having a plan is similar to doing your work wearing blindfolds and wondering if you did a good job or not.

2. **Being An Innovator**: There are going to be a lot of changes in our lifetimes. Social media is one of the many big changes that has already taken place in our lifetimes. In addition, there is nothing stopping you from creating the next big thing. How are you going to respond to and create innovations so you can give your customers the best experience they could possibly ask for?

3. **Time Management**: While you have all of these great ideas, it is important to manage your time properly so you can implement all of those ideas. Time management will give you the "I can" mindset which is essential for success.

4. **The Ability To Take Leaps**: There will be some ideas that will work, but there will be other ideas that flop. The only way to find out whether your idea is a good one or a flop is by trying it. Some ideas will involve taking risks, and that is when you will have to take leaps of faith. Are you willing to take the leap if you knew taking those leaps could make you successful?

5. **Creativity**: You need to be better than the competition by being different in order to get noticed by a lot of people. What creative services, products, and giveaways can you think of? Is there anything else creative that you can think of for your business?

6. **Consistency**: Success is not final. In order to keep your success going, you need to be consistent. What are the things that you are consistently doing, and what are the things that you are inconsistent at?

7. **The Ability To Know What Is Important**. There are a lot of options that we will be presented with. However, some options are more important than others. In order to lead the stampede, you need to know the most important parts of your business so you can enhance them and lead.
8. **Persistence**: There will be points when continuing is going to get tough. In order to keep on going, you need persistence. If you stick with it, you can end up emerging as a leader of your stampede.
9. **The Ability To Make Connections**. There are people in your niche who can give you more traffic and visibility. Interacting with the right people can result in more people knowing about you.
10. **Credibility**. In order to be taken seriously, you need to have credibility. Any future book a bestselling author writes also happens to be a very popular book. The person with 100,000 Twitter followers looks like a better social media expert than the person with 50,000 Twitter followers. Credibility allows you to lead the stampede.
11. **The Desire To Become Successful.** In order to become the leader in your niche, you need to have a desire for success right from the start. This desire for success will give you the fuel you need to bring your ideas forward.
12. **The Love For What You Do.** If you love what you do, you will not work a single day in your life. By loving what you do, you will be productive instead of busy.

Throughout *Lead The Stampede*, there will be examples of people and businesses who exhibited these characteristics and used them to lead their respective stampedes. The more you utilize these characteristics, the more likely you are to lead.

# Good Planning

The first characteristic of people who lead their stampede is good planning. This is the step that many people forget. We have been taught that starting is better than over thinking the process. While this is true, many people think that starting right away means not coming up with any kind of plan.

An unplanned product creates average results at best. An unplanned product does not allow you to build credibility and create a bestselling product. A planned product is something completely different. Planning a product, business idea, and anything else consists of many steps. For a product, the design, marketing strategy, dedicating time to complete the product, and getting testimonials are some of the planning processes that are needed to create a product that sells. Planning for success tends to bring forth success. Plan your way to success instead of rushing to the starting line.

## Time Management And Goals

Time management and goals are very important towards success. In fact, effective time management is one of the characteristics of leaders. All you need to know about time management and goals for now is that they give you a sense of direction. The goals are your compass that allow you to know where you are heading. Time management will allow you to get those goals accomplished.

One of the best ways to accomplish your goals is by having a scorecard. You can measure how effectively you are accomplishing your goals by keeping score. We all pay attention to the score of a sports game, and watching a sports game without knowing the score would be unbearable. When I use a scorecard, I write a goal down and use a tally system to figure out how close I am to accomplishing a certain goal. If I have to write 20 blog posts in 1 week, I use a tally system to get from 1 blog post to 20 blog posts. Then, I draw a big checkmark in front of all of the goals I have accomplished.

Here is what that would look like:

| Goal | Tally |
|---|---|
| Write 20 Blog Posts √ | 卌 卌 卌 卌 |

This is just an idea of how you can use goals as a compass and use effective time management to accomplish those goals. Time management and goals will be covered in greater detail later in this book.

**Using Customer Statistics As A Guide**
One of the most underrated sources of information is statistics. In *Big Data Marketing*, there are numerous statistics that dictate how customers act. One of the statistics indicated that 85% of customers would pay a higher price for a product that could get the job done better. Customers are willing to pay more money to get a higher

quality product. Although for the most part this does not apply to fast food restaurants, people are willing to pay someone $100 extra if that person can do the job (designing a website, coding an app for you) better than the other competitors.

This one statistic is very important because it tells us what customers want. Another powerful statistic mentioned in *Big Data Marketing* is that 33% of customers "showroom" which in this case means going to a retail store, seeing the product, and finding the most affordable price on the web. Retail stores could use these statistics to find out why someone buys a product online (special coupon, buy two get one free offer, or something else). Then, retail stores could create an offer similar to the online offer in their own physical stores in the hopes of getting more sales. Customers also love the ability to price match something at a retail store. This makes the process of getting the right product at the right price easier and quicker. Instead of buying the product on Amazon and waiting for a few days for it to arrive, customers can ask for a price match and get the product at their nearby retail store. Those are just three of the many statistics, polls, and surveys out there that allow us to see how customers behave. By identifying how customers behave, it will be easier for us to create compelling products and offers that are too good to ignore.

**Using Your Own Statistics As A Guide**
Some have more statistics than others, but we all have them. You can tell how many visitors you get, how many

sales you are getting, and who your customers are. The problem is that most people's statistics are unorganized because most people have no idea how statistics can predict future success. If a blog sees a 500% increase in traffic in 1 day, you can continue seeing that result by continuing to implement the tactics that got you the 500% increase in traffic. If sending 30 pins in 1 day allowed you to go from 20 daily blog visitors to 100 daily blog visitors, sending out 30 more pins tomorrow usually results in an identical or very similar result. Then, you are getting 80 extra daily blog visitors. That's almost 30,000 extra daily visitors every year. Small numbers do add up to something that is big, extraordinary, and powerful.

Statistics remain consistent if you continue to perform the same methods with the same audience. Tweeting once to 100 followers every day is going to result in some traffic from Twitter. If you are sending out 1 tweet to exactly 100 followers every month, there are going to be small, unnoticeable changes to the statistics. The average daily visitors you get from Twitter might be two daily visitors. There will be some days when you get zero visitors from Twitter, but there will be other days when you get five visitors from Twitter. There is not going to be a big change that results in all 100 of your followers suddenly deciding to visit your blog. The only way to get more people to visit your blog from Twitter is to change something. Instead of sending out one tweet, send out two tweets. You may end up averaging five daily visits to your blog. If you go from 100 followers to 1,000 followers, you may end up averaging more visitors. As you gain more followers on Twitter and send out more tweets on a consistent, frequent basis, you will get more visitors from Twitter.

Your statistics are trying to tell you the secrets to your business. Your statistics tell you why certain things are better than others. Reviewing your statistics has the potential to reveal your customers' demographics and ages, how you can get more traffic, and how you can get more followers. Then, you can learn from your statistics and implement the tactics that brought forth the best results.

**The Powers Of A Notebook**
It was not until high school when I decided to create a notebook for my business. This notebook has some of my current statistics as well as projected statistics. One of my projected statistics identified what I would need to do to get over 1,000 people to visit my blog every day. By implementing the tactics and building my following, I ended up getting over 1,000 visitors on my blog in 1 day, and it has continued ever since.

I also write calculations of how many books I would have to sell in order to make $1,000. For my books at $2.99, I make $2.04 per sale. That means I would have to sell 491 books to make $1,000. The calculations are not to the exact penny, but they give me an idea of what I have to do in order to make a certain income. I don't base my income by chance and hope to end up with a good number. I define what I would have to do to reach a desired income and do everything I can to obtain and maintain that income.

A notebook has also proven to be a very inspirational part of my journey. Before the notebook, I thought that making $10,000+ a month would be unrealistic. However, writing down the statistics allowed me to find out how many sales it would take to make that much money on a monthly basis. Giving myself defined standards gave me something to strive for.

In addition, I write my strategies in my notebook. When I think of a marketing tactic, I write it down in my notebook and think of a way to apply that tactic to my products. Mike Michalowicz wrote an entire blog post in which he mentioned a powerful marketing tactic. Michalowicz would give away his book for free with a personal letter in exchange for an honest review. As the reviews built up, Michalowicz's book, *The Pumpkin Plan*, ended up becoming a bestseller. Brendan Burchard gives free copies of his books for anyone who buys his training course. I decided to implement these tactics in my marketing strategy. I gave some people a free coupon to my Udemy training course in exchange for an honest review. Although I only offered this option to five people, I got two extra reviews (both five star reviews). Getting a free product will entice someone to give that product a five star review. That is one of the reasons *The Pumpkin Plan* has many 5 star reviews. That is also a reason why Michalowicz's other bestseller, *Toilet Paper Entrepreneur*, has over 500 reviews. By writing down these two tactics in my notebook and creating a plan that implemented those tactics, I was able to create a recipe for success. All I had to do was implement this recipe for success (which I did).

A notebook allowed me to see that success was not as hard to attain as it had always seemed to be. Before writing in the notebook, I was making an okay income which was not bad for a 14 year old but would not be as good for an adult who has to pay more expenses. I wanted to turn what I was doing into a full-time income, and writing my plan in my notebook allowed me to create a path towards that success.

## Have A Prototype

The strategy you write down in your notebook is an example of a prototype. The prototype will give you an idea of what everything should look like when your plan finally works. If you have a prototype for a book, write the name of the book on a piece of paper with your name underneath. That is what the cover of the book could look like. That is your prototype.

Having a prototype is the best way to plan because you can look at the prototype and find ways to improve upon it when you start. The prototype will serve as a powerful source of inspiration because you have a tangible product. Having a copy of *Lead The Stampede* and my other paperbacks on my desk serve as a powerful source of motivation. There is no such thing as having too much motivation. The more motivation you have, the better.

**Starting**
Planning is the most underrated step towards being successful. However, creating a plan is not enough. Your plan cannot take too long to create because then it will never reach the market. You need to create an effective plan that you can successfully implement. Creating the plan is the second hardest part of the process. Starting and choosing to turn the plan on paper into a reality is the hardest part of the process. Choosing to start and take the leap is a scary thing to do. However, there are many rewards that come from starting. There are millionaires and billionaires on our planet, and they all got to where they are today by starting. Starting is the hardest but also the most important step of the process. Planning ahead makes the process of starting much easier. Planning gives you the compass you need to sail on the seas and reach your destination.

**Planning Gives You Direction**
By creating a plan, you will give yourself a powerful sense of direction. You will have an idea of where you are heading and what the results of your actions will be. Most plans do not work perfectly, but having a plan allows you to work more effectively. Having a plan will allow you to give yourself standards to accomplish instead of guessing whether you did a good job or not.
Many successful people created plans for what their companies, products, and sales tactics should look like before they get implemented. These people ended up

creating thriving, remarkable ideas that we continue to talk about to this day. Start planning today and see what you can create.

# Being An Innovator

In a world that is rapidly changing, products and services need to be innovative to catch our attention. Whether the innovation is a change in price or a new design, it has the power to attract more customers. The person selling the video game for $40 is an innovator in the video game market. The pioneers, or the people who react the quickest, are the ones who benefit the most from the innovation. The first few people who decide to charge $40 for their video games will get the benefit as well. As long as they are among the first people to start implementing the tactic after it is proven to be successful, they will get similar results to the first person who implemented the tactic. The chances of one of the first few people succeeding is very high.

Mark Zuckerberg was one of the first people who responded to the wave of social media. When MySpace was the big thing (wait, MySpace was a big thing), Zuckerberg came out with Facebook which quickly became MySpace's superior. By effectively and quickly responding to the innovation of social media, Zuckerberg launched the multi-billion dollar social network and business, Facebook. If Zuckerberg responded too late, Facebook's chances of success may have been less likely.

The first people who respond to the innovation are the ones who usually become the most successful. However, most people in the stampede are the late birds. The late birds are the ones who respond late in the game. The late birds success rate is lower since the stampede has grown in size, but success is always a possibility. In fact, some of the late birds end up leading their own stampedes of established experts.

The way late birds respond to an innovation depends on how other people have used it to become successful. In order for late birds to be successful, they need to further differentiate themselves from the competition. Chances are that by the time the late bird joins the stampede, there are already established experts and very successful people. By mimicking the results of the successful people and implementing your own methods at the same time, you will move up in the stampede. By only mimicking the results of the successful people, most people get stuck in the middle of the stampede. Moving up proves to be difficult since a lot of the people in the middle of the stampede are doing the same thing. You need to find your secret ingredient and implement it.

In the video game example, everyone in the middle of the stampede sells the video game for $40. In order to be different and move up in the stampede, being different is key. One person decides to sell a video game for $40 and have a *Buy 1 and Get 20% Off The Second One*. For this example, people are given the ability to get two video games for $72 which is lower than the competition. People pay attention to the seller with the discount, and that person moves up in the stampede.

Not everything comes down to price though. It is possible to charge a $60 video game and still move up in the stampede. The three components of the business world are quality, price, and convenience. A business will never have all three of these components. There are few businesses that even have 2 of the 3 components. In order to move up in the stampede, you need to pick whether your business and your products are going to get sales and attention based on quality, price, or convenience.

The person with the *Buy 1 Get 20% Off The Second One* deal is focusing on the price. A lower price will lead to a larger volume of sales. Would you buy a sneaker that cost $100 or would you buy that same sneaker for $60 at another store? Many people are willing to go to the other store to save the $40 even if the store with the $100 sneakers is a two minute walk away while the store with the $60 sneakers is a 30 minute drive away. The low price gets people to go from the close store to the store that is farther away.

Another way to focus on your price is offering something for free. Who doesn't love free? A day after my Twitter Domination Training Course came out, it got over 200 signups. The Twitter Domination Training Course was my first training course ever on Udemy. I was able to get 200 signups in one day because I offered the training course for free for a limited time. By the time the free coupon expired, the training course got over 500 signups. Free products do very well because everyone wants them.

Now, that training course is no longer listed as free, and I rely on the quality (my videos) and convenience (the ability to answer anyone's question within 24 hours) to bring in sales. My Twitter Domination Training Course did have all three components of a business: quality, price, and convenience.

However, if my Twitter Domination Training Course was always listed as free, I wouldn't be making a profit. The quality and convenience would still be there, but there would be no incentive to keep the quality or convenience going. If my Twitter Domination Training Course was always free, and I didn't have another training course, that would be a big problem.

I occasionally create coupons for my training course, but there won't be any 100% off coupons anymore. Any other 100% off coupons wouldn't last nearly as long and be available to as many people as the first one.

Due to the niches some people are in, offering a free product may not be an option. While offering a free digital product does not cost you any money, it costs money to ship a physical product. Offering that physical product for free results in a profit loss. If you are in this situation, but you still want to get the benefit of offering something for free, you can offer your customers a free gift each time they purchase something. If your purchase on Lego's website is greater than $75, they give you a free gift. Some customers on Lego's website will be close to completing their $65 order but see the free gift for customers who make a purchase greater than $75. This entices people to buy an extra Lego Set to get the free prize. It's pure marketing genius.

If you have a customer service line that gets questions answered within minutes, that's convenient for the customer. When your clients have questions, they know you are reliable, so they go to you. The convenience is that you answer as quickly as possible. Going back to the analogy I made earlier, the store with the $100 sneakers is convenient because it is nearby. The price isn't there, but the convenience is. Some consumers focus on quality (how good a product is), some consumers focus on the price (how low the price is), and some consumers focus on the convenience (the "make my life easier" decision).

You need to decide which components of the business world you will be known for. Brendan Burchard has a lot of quality videos in his training course about creating lucrative products. The only catch is that the training course costs $1,997 to access. Brendan Burchard focuses on quality and convenience (unless the training course is closed and you wanted to join), but having a low price is not one of the components of the business world that Burchard focuses on.

There are a lot of commercials about discounts for cars. The low price will get people's attention. There are other people who cruise the streets in a Lamborghini. Those cars are very expensive, and they take about a year to make (no assembly line, just people). However, the quality of the Lamborghini is ensured. In a *60 Minutes* interview about the Lamborghini, one person driving in another car next to the Lamborghini stopped the car just to take a picture of the Lamborghini. The Lamborghini is the dream car for many people because of the quality: how it looks and its speed. The price tag doesn't encourage people to buy the car because some of those price tags can be very expensive. There are three Lamborghinis that cost $4 million *each*. People buy these cars because of the quality.

You need to decide whether you will be remarkable for the quality, price, or convenience of your products or services. Think carefully as you choose which one you will commit to because by consistently implementing one or sometimes two of the three options, people will know you for quality, price, or convenience. Let's go into some of the results associated with choosing quality, price, convenience, or a mix of the two.

**Quality**
Quality is the component that numerous people strive for. The mental mindset is, "I put in a lot of work to create this product. I am going to charge a lot." These people think that by creating a quality product, the price tag won't matter as much. Most of the quality products happen to also be the most expensive ones. The problem with quality is that it requires more work than all of the other options. If you want to be known for quality, you have to put in 110% of your effort into creating your products. Your product needs to be the cream of the crop in order to focus on quality.

Clients who have never used your services before or bought your products will be reluctant towards buying a product with a big price tag. People don't know you for the quality until they buy your product, read your blog posts, watch one of your videos, or hear about you in a good way. Once you get noticed, making sales will be easier, and you will be the superstar of your niche who leads your niche's stampede.

## Price

Price is another component that people strive for. Some people offer big discounts, or their products are the least expensive products of their niche. The price aspect will allow you to get a volume sales. Would you rather buy something for $40, or would you rather buy something for $20 that isn't as good as the $40 product? Different people will have different answers depending on what those products are and what those people seek. Some people go to fast food restaurants while others grab a bite to eat at more expensive restaurants.

Target and WalMart have lower prices than their competitors which is why those big chains of stores are around. Target and WalMart focus on price. People look for discounts, especially on Black Friday when the holidays approach. Having a product with a lower price will encourage a greater volume of sales.

Before you decide to follow this method, understand that lower prices do not mean better products. The only thing low prices do are get a greater volume of sales. By getting a greater volume of sales, people will know more about you. As the saying goes, it's better for the seller if 10 people buy a $5 product than it is if 1 person buys a $40 product. The seller makes an extra $10 with the volume of sales. By lowering the price, your commission for each sale will not be as large, but you will get more sales with a lower price.

**Convenience**

Convenience is how quickly you respond to an email, how good your customer service is, how quickly you can deliver a product, how close your store is to someone's house (if you want a store), and giving people control of your schedule. Convenience is something that people are reluctant to do because giving people control of your schedule sounds really bad. When you first start your business, chances are you won't have enough money to hire a customer service team. For the first months of your business, you will be the person who has to constantly adjust your schedule in order to meet your clients' needs. Your clients will love you for giving them the convenience that they need. By being there for your client, they are more likely to buy your products and tell other people about you. Now, you have to adapt your schedule to the needs of more people. As you adapt your schedule to the needs of more people, your profit will increase. Soon enough, you will have enough money to hire someone to help out with the responses. Hiring someone to help you respond to customers will cut down the amount of time you respond to customers' questions significantly. As you continue to make a bigger profit, you will gain the power to hire more people to help your clients.

In order to be convenient, you need to change your schedule numerous times. However, convenience can be systematized. By hiring a lot of people, you can have them be convenient to your clients while you don't have to change your schedule nearly as much as before. The beginning is a very bumpy one, but convenience can be systematized.

**Quality And Price: The Underpricing Method**
There are a lot of people who don't support the underpricing method. If you underprice your product, chances are that someone will tell you that you made the wrong decision. When I charged $2.99 for my book, *How To Be Successful On Twitter*, people who knew me well urged me to raise the price.

The underpricing method will face some opposition from you or some of the people you know who see you underpricing your product. The underpricing method is a risk because it lowers your profit, and you put in a lot of work to create the product. Instead of making a $10 profit per sale, you may only end up making a $5 profit per sale. Here's why the underpricing method has worked: the low price leads to a higher volume of sales. Instead of making 25 sales every month with a higher priced product, you are making 100 sales every month with a lower priced product. The difference that makes in a year is incredible. The person who makes 25 sales every month ends up making 300 sales every year while the person who makes 100 sales every month ends up making 1200 sales every year. Even if the person with 300 sales makes the same or greater profit than the person who makes 1200 sales, here's the benefit:

Statistics show that 90% of sales come from returning customers, 9% of sales come from people who got referred, and 1% of sales are a result of someone who just happens to find you. Getting 1,200 people to buy your product will allow it to spread faster than if only 300 people bought your product. When word of mouth comes into the equation, the person who made a greater volume of sales will be noticed by more people. More people will notice the person who underprices their product than the person who charges overpriced ones.

The advantage of having the quality is that when you get enough sales, you will eventually become the superstar of your niche and lead the stampede. You will be able to become the superstar of your niche faster by underpricing your product because you will get a greater volume of sales. More people will know about your quality product in a quicker amount of time. You will be able to lead the stampede faster with the underpricing method.

### Quality and Convenience: The Ultimate Client Satisfaction Method

By combining quality and convenience, you will be able to give your clients the satisfaction that they need. In fact, your clients will be so satisfied that they will be more likely to tell their friends about your products and services. By creating quality products and giving your clients the top-level convenience, they will be very impressed with you. When your clients realize your product is really good, they will be eager to buy all of your products and spread the word. All you have to do is create another product, and then it will automatically get more sales.

Out of all of the combinations, the Ultimate Client Satisfaction Method requires the most work. You have to put in a lot of work and effort when it comes to creating your products. In addition to that, you will also have to constantly respond to your clients on a timely basis. That requires a lot of time, work, and commitment, and when you hire people to help out, you have to make sure they are going to do a good job as well.

The money you make from selling your quality products will allow you to hire more people. The convenience part does get systematized, but in order to pay for all of the quality employees, you need to spend some of the money you bring in. In the end, this strategy will work out in your favor because hiring qualified people will free your time to focus on creating more quality products that can bring in more revenue.

**Price and Convenience: The Volume Method**
The Volume Method will allow you to gain a greater volume of clients. This will result in more sales which will boost your profit. By having a low price, more people will come to you for the convenience. Your list of clients will grow, and you will be responding to more customers before your income will be strong enough to hire employees. Since The Volume Method is based on price and convenience, you can hire virtual assistants who are able to do the job right. The assistants you hire should be able to respond within 24 hours. Hiring more people will boost the chances of a customer getting a response within 24 hours. In addition,

you will have more control of your schedule when you are following The Volume Method before hiring anyone.
This method should result in a big volume of clients, but it is important to remember that not all clients are created equal. Identify your top clients and put in the quality to attract those clients. Everyone else may have to wait a little longer, but if your top clients don't have to wait very long, they will feel special.
You will find your quality clients faster and get more sales. In order to be successful with The Volume Method, you need to establish who your top clients are and focus on them. As you start to make a profit, hire other people to respond to the new clients and the second tier clients.
When a new client becomes a top client, directly responding to that person will make that client happier to do business with you (and buy more of your products because of the personal interaction).
In addition to the convenience not taking up as much time, you will get a volume of sales since your products aren't expensive. People are more willing to spend $5 than they are to spend $10. People will find that the price is very convenient, and when you continue to be convenient to your clients, they will buy your other products as well.

**Choose The One That Works For You**
Quality, price, convenience, and their combinations are the options you have to creating a successful business.
Maintaining all three of those options in one business plan is impossible, but if you get a combination or focus on one

of the three, your business will be able to soar. In order to lead the stampede, you need to identify which one works for you as quickly as possible. If you want to focus on one of the three options without focusing on any of the other options, that's entirely okay. If you want to focus on one of the combinations, that is also okay. You may find that implementing a combination may require too much work or isn't as rewarding as it should be. You may find that you work really well by implementing one of the three options. As long as you identify which of these options or combinations you will implement for your business, you are getting closer to the front of the stampede. By implementing the decision and accomplishing the goal, you will be able to catch up to the people who are at the front of the stampede.

**After You Make Your Choice**
After you decide among quality, price, convenience, or a mix of the two, you need to become really good and well-known for what you choose. If you chose quality, you need to take steps of action to make yourself known for quality. Some of these steps of action could be creating quality products, having quality content, and other forms of quality that will allow you to stand out from the crowd. All of the successful people who are at the front of the stampede are efficient at managing their time. In the next part of *Lead The Stampede*, I will show you what you need to know so you can improve your time management. By improving your time management, you will be able to respond to innovation

faster than everyone else and come up with the ideas, products, and content that shine.

## The Ability To Innovate

The people who lead their stampedes are able to effectively respond to innovation. What establishes the leaders of the stampede from the people not far behind is the ability to innovate. Social media was an innovation. Mark Zuckerberg was able to innovate, and now Facebook is one of the many social networks on the web. Jeff Bezos was innovative as well, and now Amazon is the leader of e-commerce. Mark Zuckerberg and Jeff Bezos are leading their stampedes because they were innovative at the right time.

## Timing

If Zuckerberg launched Facebook 10 years later, someone else would probably have the leading social network. If Bezos launched Amazon 10 years later, someone else would probably be the leader of e-commerce. In order to be innovative and create something that grabs attention, timing is crucial. If you are too late, someone will come up with the innovation before you do. In order to get the right timing, you need to innovate at the right time. The two ways to innovate at the right time is by thinking of and implementing the innovative idea before everyone else or to make one idea that already exists completely different but attractive at the same time.

## Thinking Of The Idea

Remember when there was no web? I don't. When the web first came, it was an empty market. There are currently millions of people on the web competing for attention, but when the web was new, people were not competing on it. Everything on the web started as an idea including email, blogging, online training courses, social networks, e-learning, Google, online videos, and everything else. It seems as if everyone wishes they thought of Google, Facebook, and all of the other big names and ideas. Those ideas are taken, but there is a way to hack the system so your idea is the next innovative one. You may not be able to create a search engine like Google, but you may be able to create something that becomes as well-known as Google. The thought of your idea being as well-known as Google sounds farfetched, but with the right idea, your innovative idea can be as innovative as Google.

The best way to think of an innovative idea is to think of answers to society's problems. That may have sounded like something from your History textbook, but that is how ideas such as Google became well-known. Google solved the need of going to the library to do research so the essay could be finished. People can now find all of the information they need by searching something on Google. Facebook solved the problem of friends looking for a way to connect with each other and stay in touch. The telephone did solve the problem, but Facebook solved the problem even better. Friends from New York and California can now talk to each other and send pictures to each other. Instead of calling 10 people with a telephone to relay the same message, one Facebook post will do the job for you. Communicating with others has been made a lot easier.

Online training courses have allowed more people to become teachers and reach more students easier. A teacher from South Africa can now teach students in the Americas. E-learning services also benefit because they make revenue each time any training course on the service makes a sale. Udemy may have been a late bird in this area, but it is now leading the stampede.

Blogs have allowed more people to write what is on their mind. Blogging revolutionized what it meant to be known for quality content. Before blogs, the only way to become well-known for quality content was by being an author or a writer for a popular newspaper like *The New York Times*. Blogging has allowed many unknown writers to become prominent writers and authors in their niche. Since WordPress did the best job at responding to the innovation, they're leading the stampede.

3D printing has allowed people to print 3D objects and thus change the way manufacturing works. Unknown manufacturers can now use 3D printing to become well-known. Just like blogs, 3D printers have allowed the unknown to become well-known. That is one of the problems society faces: people want their products to be offered to the world. 3D printers and training course creators such as Udemy are two of the tools that some individuals use to solve this problem.

There are even more ways to solve the same problem. Some geometry problems can be solved in over 20 different ways. 3D printers and blogs both solved the same problem for some individuals. There are still some people who want to go from unknown to well-known who can't do that with a blog or a 3D printer. There are other ways to go from unknown to well-known, but this is definitely a problem that many people have.

There are a lot of problems in today's society. Shopping has been a problem. Some people want to buy products for the lowest price while others go for the high-end products with higher prices. There are many websites such as Points2Shop now with point systems that allow you to get products for free (I have tried Points2Shop, and they deliver on the promise).

In order to think of an idea, you need to identify a problem. You may be experiencing a problem that you want a solution for. Instead of waiting for someone else to come up with the solution, you can come up with the solution. Chances are there will be other people with the same problem, and if you solve the problem for yourself, you will benefit. Not only do you solve the problem for yourself, but you can also create a business that helps people solve that particular problem. Some businesses based on solving other people's problems have turned into multimillion dollar enterprises.

## It's Not As Challenging As It Sounds

There are some people who think of innovations that could rival Facebook. For most of us, thinking of an innovation that could rival Facebook is a daunting task. Making an innovation does not always mean creating something completely new. Creating an innovation can also mean a small innovation. These are small innovations that we could have thought of and done. Oracle Cards became successful by selling card decks that had inspirational messages on every card. Creating small innovations is not as challenging as it sounds.

## How A Small Innovation Resulted In Fusion Tour

There are countless networking events, and it is getting more difficult than ever for new networking events to thrive and rise above the competition. Vernetta Freeney is one of the many people who goes to networking events. However, Vernetta realized that after many networking events, she would leave with no connections. The networking events turned out to just waste her time.

Vernetta decided to solve the problem by creating her own networking event called Fusion Tour. The idea for Fusion Tour came from reading the book, *Wicked Success Is Inside Every Woman* by Vickie L. Millazzo. As an introvert, it was hard for Vernetta to walk up to strangers and begin a conversation. To solve that problem (killing two birds with one stone), Vernetta created an event where she invited people that she wanted to learn more about. This allowed Vernetta and the invited networkers to learn more about one another and see how their businesses could support each other. A brilliant idea was born.

Since then, Fusion Tour has launched over 20 collaborations, partnerships, projects, and more in just three years. Several women who have attended Fusion Tour have been featured in national magazines. Women who attend Fusion Tour share their ideas with each other and then implement the feedback they got about their specific idea.

Fusion Tour is the atmosphere for women entrepreneurial introverts to create authentic connections and create a collaborative, connected community to help each other's businesses soar. Fusion Tour allows these entrepreneurs to find specific connections and resources, and then use these connections and resources to strengthen their brand message and presence in their niche.

**Implementing The Idea**

Thinking of the idea is the easy part. Implementing that idea and turning it into a reality is the challenging part. You may have already thought of the idea that will solve a lot of people's problems or make something easier. Implementing the idea requires work, and most people want to avoid the work.

Instead of creating something remarkable, many people decide to play it safe. In order to implement the remarkable idea, a lot of time will have to be dedicated towards that idea. That time can be utilized on the tactics that are already working. Many people go through the 9 to 5 routine because the routine brings in money. The routine can be a bit hectic, but it brings in revenue. The 9 to 5 routine is safe. In order to lead the stampede, you need to leave safe behind. It takes courage, guts, determination, and other factors to decide that you want to lead a stampede of your own. Too many people are playing it safe. I would go as far to say that millions of people are playing it safe, and standing out when you are just like a million other people will not work out very well. Therefore, safe is not safe. In fact, it's dangerous. The leaders of the stampede got there by taking leaps between cliffs while everyone else stayed on the safe ground, not moving forward when the going got tough. If you have a day job, you should find some hours outside of the job to work on your big idea.

Your idea may be a risky one. Apple was a risky idea that almost went bankrupt. It may require a lot of money to pull it off or a big learning curve on your part. However, your idea has the potential to turn into something remarkable. If you have faith in your idea, and you keep working on it, your idea will be able to thrive, but only after the idea gets implemented. You need to start before you can finish. There is no way around it. Once you see the finished product, you will be able to marvel at what you have created.

The finished product is what we all look at. Many people forget about the work it takes to go from start to finish. We all forget how much work it took for Amazon to become an empire. When people start to do the work required to turn their idea into a reality, they become afraid. They realize this is going to take more time than was expected. Don't let the fear stop you. Fight through it. The leaders do have fear, but they have the courage to persevere and fight against fear.

Motivation is essential for anything that you do in life because motivation gives you the drive to go farther and beyond. Earlier in this book, I talked about motivation for time management. Now I am going to talk about motivation when it comes to implementing your ideas.

Just like time management, you need to have a vision to turn your idea into a reality. This time, only create a vision that revolves around your specific idea. Where do you see yourself after you implement your idea? Do you see yourself as a well-known person of your niche who leads the stampede? Write down what you see in your vision and read it before, while, and after you are working on the implementation process of your idea.

Motivation is something that we need to constantly have and be reminded of. Constantly remind yourself of your vision. While you are working, constantly remind yourself of why you are working on your idea and what it can become. What is turning this idea into a reality going to accomplish? By reminding yourself of your purpose, and giving yourself the extra push with the vision, you will be able to turn your idea into a reality.

The marketplace only rewards the ideas that get implemented. The market can only know about you if you decide to turn your idea into a reality. There are a lot of people who think of powerful ideas, but since those ideas don't get implemented, we don't get to know about them. In order to go from unknown to well-known, you need to implement your innovative ideas.

Waiting for someone to find us and show us the way is not an option. We need to create our own paths. We need to solve our own problems so we can indirectly solve the problems of thousands or even millions of people. There are a lot of problems out there, but if you find the solution to a common problem, you are going to become well-known for finding the answer. There are a lot of rewards that you will get once your idea becomes a reality. People will write about your idea, share it with other people, and your idea will become the next big thing.

Some of the problems that have been solved are very similar to problems that have not been solved yet. The thinking associated with solving 2+2 is similar to the thinking process of solving 20+20. That way, all you need to do is apply the original idea to another problem and tinker around with it. ManageFlitter allows its users to manage all of their followers and unfollow the people who are not following them back. However, there is not a tool that allows you to do that for Pinterest (I'm going to ask for 5% if you make that happen). ManageFlitter solved the problem for Twitter users, and it can be used as an excellent guideline to solve the same exact problem that is presented on Pinterest. In some cases, all you have to do is convert something in order to implement an innovative idea that sticks.

In order to implement an idea, you need to create a schedule and add that idea to your schedule. You need to add non-negotiable hours, certain hours throughout the week in which you will spend some of your time working on your idea in an uninterrupted fashion. At what time each day will you work on your idea? Will you work on your idea more on Tuesdays than on Thursdays? Those are the types of questions you need to ask yourself as you create your schedule. When you create your schedule, consider all of the other tasks and goals you have to accomplish. Make sure you have enough time to work on the tasks and goals while working on the big idea. Your other work can't fall behind as you focus on your big idea, but you need enough time in the day in order to effectively accomplish the big idea.

**Everyone Started From The Bottom**
Every bestselling author started out with no followers, no sales, and no book. Every sales rep started out with no referrals and no customers. Every blogger started out with no visitors, no subscribers, and no sales. Every power user on Twitter started out with zero followers, zero tweets, and an egg as a profile image. Everyone who started, from the current leaders to the aspiring leaders, started at the back of the stampede.
Not everyone from the bottom makes it to the top, but what is stopping you from breaking that low standard? In order to get to the top, you need to implement your ideas and be innovative. The people who are one of a kind get the most sales, publicity, and attention in their respective niches.

In order to get more attention and get closer to the front of the stampede, people need to notice you. The main way people get noticed is by being unique. Some leaders have unique stories. Other leaders do one thing very well. Other leaders are known as the nice people of their niche. In order to go from the bottom to the top, you need to be noticed for something that few people or no one else does. In order to do that, you need to innovate.

**The Main Problem For People Who Join New Niches**
3D printing is revolutionary, and it's creating the shiny syndrome effect. The ability to become one of the first people to start something completely new is a rare opportunity. If 3D printing was not as popular as it is today, and you had the opportunity to be one of the first people to use a 3D printer, would you have taken that opportunity? The main problem associated with taking leaps out of your niche is that you now have to learn new things about the new niche. In addition, when a new niche starts out, its success is uncertain. The 3D printing niche did end up becoming a big success, but what if it was a giant flop. I am sure there are people who could not possibly imagine 3D printing being a giant flop, but there have been businesses that looked like the next big thing but ended up flopping instead.
In addition, critics find anyway to make a product look like a failure. Critics never thought planes would be successful. Critics thought that the television would never be successful because people would not want to sit still and stare at a

screen all day. Those criticisms proved to be inaccurate considering that the average American watches 32 hours of television every week (I'm not the average American though). We don't know much about those critics because they are long gone. When the idea works, the critics vanish, but when the idea isn't popular yet, critics are everywhere. Some people become a part of a new niche and become successful. This is the exception, not the rule. If you want to pursue a new niche, understand that you will have to learn new things about that new niche. However, you do not have to be a part of an innovative niche in order to be innovative. 3D printing is an innovative niche because it is the new technology that can do something that was previously impossible. Shapeways has a powerful video that shows exactly how powerful 3D printing is and how far it has already come. Being innovative can also mean staying in the niche you are currently in and making some changes to that niche. When you make the innovations to your niche, you are still the expert, and if your innovations are really good, you will plunge ahead of the competition. All you need to do is keep on doing what you have already been doing, and the competition won't be able to keep up to your standard of excellence.

## When The Competition Catches Up...
When you do something new in your niche that works, the competition will do everything it can to catch up. Some of the competitors will catch up to you and go for the leading spot in the stampede. When the competition catches up,

many people decide to make big changes. The thinking process is that the big changes will allow them to stand out from the crowd and lead the stampede yet again without anyone challenging them.

The problem with making big changes is that those big changes have the potential to change a business' identity. Changing the identity of a successful business spells out trouble because the loyal customers won't know what to think. The go-to business just changed its identity and its entire branding structure. The thinking process for the business may shift from treating quality clients at a higher standard to trying to get a quantity of clients without focusing on quality clients. The identity change results in former loyal customers looking for other businesses that have an identity that they are looking for.

When the competition catches up, it is important to make small changes instead of big changes. The small changes that matter to the customers will get noticed while your business still keeps its identity and those loyal customers. Sometimes a big change may be necessary, but a big change that changes the identity of your brand is typically not worth the work or time.

**Be Innovative With Your Time**

The difference between success and failure is not how much time you have, but how you are using that time. In order to be successful, you need to use your time in an effective manner. Doing one or two things differently with the time you have may be the difference between making no sales and making over a million sales in a short period of time. Time is the most valuable resource we have. There are many ways to enrich that resource, but like all resources, there are many ways to deplete them as well. In order to lead the stampede, you need to enrich that resource. Being productive is no longer enough. Being productive and doing some things differently while getting the results you want is the right path to success.

Think of how you are utilizing your time. Know that by making some very small changes, you may end up leading the stampede by utilizing the same amount of time you have been utilizing day by day. Try to make some small changes and track how those small changes affect your results. You will be surprised with your results.

# Time Management

The best way to get goals accomplished is by having good time management skills. We all have 24 hours in a day, but not everyone is utilizing those hours properly. The leaders of the stampede properly utilize as many of those hours as possible. Many of the people at the back of the stampede tend to have poor time management skills.

In order to become an effective manager of your time, you need these three components: motivation, direction, and a purpose. The leaders of the stampede exhibit all three of these components. That is why the leaders of the stampede are very efficient at managing their time.

Think of what you would be able to accomplish if you had an extra hour in the day. Then, think of what you would be able to accomplish if you had two extra hours in the day. Leaders find the ability to manage their time by finding those extra hours in the day. In today's world, there are more ways to procrastinate for a longer amount of time than ever. There's the TV, internet, social media, YouTube videos, and Vine videos just to name a few of the distractions that result in more procrastination when they are not properly utilized. Using these platforms to procrastinate too often will prevent you from being the leader of your stampede. If you are a leader of your stampede who procrastinates too often with these platforms, imagine how much farther you could be ahead of the people in your stampede if you did not procrastinate as often—or at all.

In order to manage your time efficiently, you need to be able to reduce the amount of time you spend procrastinating. In order to reduce the amount of time you spend doing other things such as watching TV or surfing the web, reduce the time you spend daily on all of those activities by 15 minutes each week. That's 15 extra minutes you have in order to work on enhancing your business' quality, price, convenience, or mix of the two each day. As you continue carving out 15 minutes per day for seven days a week from those activities, more time will start to open up. In order to reduce the amount of time you procrastinate, you need the motivation, direction, and purpose that will allow you to get there. These three components of time management will help out big time. The motivation will allow you to keep on going. Along with the motivation comes the direction: what do you need to do. With those two components comes the purpose which is the "why" part of your mission. Why do you do what you do? I will show you how to utilize all three of these components so you become effective at managing your time.

**Motivation**
Motivation is essential for everything that you pursue. You need the motivation to stick with your mission when you encounter challenges and distractions. There are going to be some very bad days. Even the leaders experience bad days. Sometimes, a situation may look hopeless. Being motivated will allow you to see light at the end of the tunnel, hope, and prosperity despite the current situation. In the

end, motivation allows individuals to overcome their situations and rise above the difficulties if they stay motivated during their entrepreneurial journeys. In order to stay motivated, you need to give yourself a vision, goals you need to stay committed to, and a notebook.

**Your Vision**

Your vision is an important element of the motivation process. Imagine where you will be in the future. You may see yourself as a bestselling author, a leader of your stampede with a thriving business, or a role model for others to follow. Where do you want to be in the future? What are all of the things that you want to accomplish in that time? That is your vision.

In order to stay motivated, you need to have this kind of vision. I want you to get a notebook and write down everything you can think of for your vision of your desired future. Write down the short-term goals that you see yourself accomplishing in a short period of time as well as the long-term goals which may take a few months or years to pull off. If you think of yourself becoming a online trainer with 100 training courses, write that down. If you think of yourself building a multimillion dollar business, write that down too. The more details you write down for your vision, the more you will be motivated to put in the work.

Few people think about giving themselves the vision, but a vision is very motivational. Most people only *think* about what they want to become. When most people think of what they want to become, they don't *write* down what they want to become. The problem with that is the human mind can only remember so many things, and most thoughts end up becoming vague. It is entirely possible and common for thoughts to be forgotten (life happens). Instead of forgetting about great ideas, write down what you think about in a notebook. This will allow you to paint a clearer picture of your vision. When I think of something I want to become, I write it down. Another problem with only thinking about something is that you aren't fully committing yourself. If you write something in a notebook, you will be more committed towards accomplishing it. When I write a goal in my notebook, I feel more obligated towards accomplishing that goal. You will feel that same obligation to get your goals accomplished when you write them down in your notebook. Another way to strengthen your obligation towards accomplishing these goals is making yourself accountable to a certain group of people. Whether this means joining accountability groups in your niche (this can be done with a Facebook Group Page), or telling your family members what your vision is, make sure you take accountability for your vision. You can also find an accountability partner and work with that person similar to having a workout buddy. Taking accountability for your vision will make it more likely to happen since you are now making yourself responsible (no one to blame if anything goes wrong).

**How To Come Up With A Great Vision**
Not all visions are created equal. Some visions are good while others are not as good. There are three different

kinds of visions: the underachieving vision, the impossible vision, and the ideal vision.

The underachieving vision is a vision that is too easy. Getting 100 followers on a social network is not something to put in your vision because it won't take a few years to get those 100 followers. Writing a blog post should not be a part of your vision because writing a blog post is something that can be achieved in a short amount of time. Although these two tasks can be goals you use to get closer to your vision, small tasks should not be mixed up for the big vision.

An underachieving vision is one that gets fulfilled in a short amount of time. It may only take a few days or weeks to fulfill the vision. The reason an underachieving vision is not effective is because it requires minimal work. Fulfilling the vision is too easy. A vision is where you see yourself months or even years from now, but a vision is not where you see yourself days or weeks from now.

Another vision that does not work so well is the impossible vision. This vision is one with goals that are impossible to reach and require an overwhelming amount of work on your part. Getting 1 billion Twitter followers in five years is an overwhelming task. Not even the big-time celebrities are able to get 1 billion Twitter followers within five years. By overwhelming yourself with too much work, you won't be able to get all of your tasks accomplished, and your vision will have to be changed and reduced constantly. Don't give yourself a vision that is impossible to fulfill. Choosing a vision that is impossible to fulfill has the power to lower your confidence and make it more difficult for you to achieve that vision.

The right vision, the ideal vision, is one that brings forth an uncomfortable but not overwhelming amount of work. The right vision gives you a list of things you want to be and accomplish that are reachable within a few months or years. Getting 1 billion followers on Twitter is unrealistic. Getting 100,000 followers on Twitter is a possibility. Your vision should require you to take a big leap and go from where you are now to somewhere far greater.

**Dream Big**
There are going to be some things that you think of that look impossible at first but are actually very possible. Even if you think something is impossible, write it down. It is better to dream big than it is to dream too small. The process may be overwhelming after the first week, but by effectively managing your time, you may eventually turn the impossibility into a possibility.

I thought that coming out with a training course in a month was impossible. I started my training course anyway, and in 1 week, I launched my 20 video training course called Twitter Domination. Before I started the process, creating a 20 video training course in a month seemed unrealistic to me. The 20 videos I created added up to two and a half hours of content, and I got them done in well under a month.

You may think that one of your goals is impossible to reach, but I thought the same about my Twitter Domination training course. I didn't get overwhelmed with the work. I just found effective ways to manage my time so I would be able to complete the training course in a month. I was able to do 3-6 videos every day and get to 20 videos. This was a big moment for me because I realized that some of the goals I assumed were impossible were actually very possible.

I also thought I would get my 100,000th Twitter follower in 2016, my senior year of high school. In this case, I dreamed too small. I was able to reach the same milestone two years before. At the time, I thought I was dreaming big, but as I learned new skills to grow my Twitter presence, I realized that I needed to dream bigger. Based on calculations, I will easily have 400,000 Twitter followers at the same time I said I would have 100,000 Twitter followers, and I may even get to 500,000 Twitter followers within that same timeframe. This is why managing your time is critical towards success. Instead of feeling overwhelmed about the work, you can allocate yourself more time so you merely feel uncomfortable with the rate that you do the work in. Leaders of the stampede often feel uncomfortable with the amount of work they do, but this discomfort leads to urgency. In return, the urgency leads to more work getting done faster in a more productive manner.

## Direction

Once you are motivated and have the vision, you need to have direction. You get this sense of direction by identifying your goals, priorities, and big quarterly goal. The goals are what need to get done, the priorities are the goals that need to get done first, and the big quarterly goal is the most challenging goal that will take the most time to complete, but that goal will bring forth the best results.

**Goals, Priorities, And The Big Quarterly Goal**
You may have a giant list of goals you want to accomplish this quarter. If you don't have a list of goals, start writing them down. Your goals are your GPS. If you don't know where you are going, you aren't going to end up where you expected to be. Let's say you live in Texas and you wanted to drive up to California to see a Super Bowl, the world's most crooked street, or something else. It would take almost an entire day to pull it off, and one wrong turn can ruin where you end up. With a GPS, you can quickly realize you made the wrong turn and go back on course.
The goals you wrote down show you where your business needs to go. Without the goals guiding you, you will not know where you have to end up. Without the GPS, you may end up in Nevada instead of California. In a car, the GPS is shown on the car's dashboard, and metaphorically speaking, your notebook is similar to your car's dashboard. There are notebooks with multiple functions such as goal creation, doodles, and other things as well. However, you need to have a notebook entirely dedicated to your business. That's the notebook where you should be writing down all of your goals. You can get all of the directions from Google Maps, but all of that paperwork is eventually going to get scattered and lost. If you only go to California once a

year, you'll end up throwing away the Google Map directions when you get back to Texas.

Instead of throwing your lists of goals away, put them all in one place: a notebook. With a notebook, you can get more specific with your goals since you know you won't lose your list. You may have written down as a goal to make $15,000 a month. With a notebook, you can go deeper and find out which avenues of revenue will allow you to make that $15,000 a month. How much do your products have an impact? Then you can break it down to which products need to be able to make how much money to get you to your goal. How much of an impact does advertising have? Then you can break down how you use advertising on YouTube videos, your blog, and so on. You also have over 100 pages in a notebook versus one piece of paper to list your goals. Then, you better hope that that one piece of paper does not get lost in the other papers on your desk. You can get as specific with your goals as you want.

When you get specific with your goals, you are giving yourself a better plan to accomplish those goals. Let's go back to the example of making $15,000 a month. If someone only wrote down, "Make $15,000 a month," the first question I would have is, "How are you going to make that happen?"

With a notebook, you can answer that question. You can go into specific details in a way that would be impossible with a piece of paper. Your current status is Point A, your version of Texas. Making the $15,000 a month is Point B, your version of California. Being specific with that goal and creating steps on how to accomplish that goal is your GPS from Texas to California.

Your notebook will forever change the way you look at and accomplish your goals. Your notebook will organize your goals in a way that makes them look easier than ever. Your goals aren't going to be scattered any longer. People forget to accomplish their goals because the goals get lost in the process. It is important to realize that we can only remember so much information, and when we think of new goals, it is quite possible that we forget about some of the old ones. With a notebook, you can remember all of your old goals and all of the new goals that you strive to accomplish.

There are going to be people who are skeptical about writing their goals in a notebook. Some people may say that they can type their goals in a document instead of writing them in a notebook. However, you should definitely stick with the notebook because writing down your own goals by hand increases your accountability. You are going to create many documents on your computer, and that will make your list of goals harder to find and more difficult to remember. Your notebook contains all of your goals in an uncontested environment. On a computer, there are a lot of other things that can distract you and prevent you from typing your goals. You can go on the internet, check the inbox, create a KeyNote, or do something else. When you have a notebook, you can only write down goals. There aren't any distractions when it comes to writing in your notebook.

Another great reason to use a notebook is that you actually get to check off the goal when you are done. Being able to put a checkmark next to an accomplished goal releases a part of the brain that makes you feel good and boost confidence. You get this type of feeling by writing that big checkmark with a pen or pencil on paper.

There is one essential reason why you should stick with your notebook. When you type about your goals, you aren't fully committing yourself towards completing those goals. You can just hit the backspace button and all of the work you have to put in goes away. If you write your goals in pen in a notebook, there is no backspace button. You can't erase away your goals either. Even if you used whiteout, you would know that something would be missing from your plan. When you write a goal in your notebook, you are committed to accomplishing that goal. What you wrote is indelible. It cannot be removed, and if you try to remove it, you will always see that small smudge that indicates there was a goal there. You are forcing yourself to stick with your goal, implement it, accomplish it, and thrive.

In addition, it is entirely possible for a computer or a computer hard drive to crash. If this happens, you will lose all of your information, including any goals that you wrote down for yourself. Your computer may be the new up-to-date version or one of the older versions, but regardless of which computer you have, you cannot take that chance. Another great benefit with a notebook is that you can look at your past notes. If your goal was to make $15,000 every month, and you past your goal, you will be able to smile at what you wrote down knowing that you accomplished one of your goals. I remember when one of my goals was to get to 1,000 Twitter followers. I now have more than 1,000 Twitter followers. You will be able to look back at all of the goals you wrote down and remember where you were when you first wrote those goals. You will be able to remember what Point A was like when you are at Point B. Looking back at your journey is a great way to see what you have accomplished and ignite and inspire yourself towards further accomplishments.

At the beginning of every quarter, you should be writing down a list of goals in your notebook. However, your quarters don't have to start on January, April, July, or October. Your first quarter starts from the moment you fully commit to this plan. Whether you start your first quarter at the beginning of February or in the middle of June, you should be writing a list of goals in your notebook. Three months later, you'll start your next quarter where you will be able to assess what you have completed so far.

Your notebook is an important part for this plan to work. You need to be committed to accomplishing your goals, and writing your goals in your notebook will give you the commitment you need. Some of the time that you gained by giving up on forms of procrastination will be used to writing your goals in your notebook. That's just one of the many ways all of that extra time is going to help you properly execute the plan.

"Being entirely honest with oneself is a good exercise." -- Sigmund Freud

The only way for this plan to work is if you are honest with yourself. We all want to believe that we do everything perfectly, but we don't. There are going to be some really productive days when you get everything done for the day and do extra work as well. There will be some unproductive days when the marathon of your favorite show is on or when you go on a road trip. However, it's very important that you are honest with yourself.

The best way to be honest with yourself is by writing these questions in your notebook each week and answering them *honestly*:

1. **How much have I done for my business this week?** If you're doing a lot for your business, then you're on the right track.
2. **Did I get my weekly milestones accomplished?** If they weren't accomplished, what was/were the main reason(s)? Doing a lot for your business in a week is good, but are you accomplishing the goals you set for yourself week by week (I'll talk about the week by week plan later in this book)?
3. **Am I finding other ways to grow my business?** You can't rely primarily on the methods you are already using to grow your business. There are other ways that work as well.

4. **Am I adding more goals to my list as the days go on?**
   Depending on how many goals were on your original list,
   you may decide to add more goals to your list.

Don't write down the best answer that makes it look as if
you put in a good amount of work; write the truthful answer
that reveals whether you put in a good amount of work
towards accomplishing your goals or not. The best answer,
but not always the honest answer, is saying that you have
done numerous tasks for your business this week even if
you know you did not get half of them done. In this
scenario, you would have to answer honestly which would
be that you were not as productive in that particular week
as you expected.

No matter how productive you are or how productive you
become, you will not be productive every week, and in
some cases, it will hurt to write the truth. Writing the truth
indicates that there are flaws, and few people want to
address their flaws. However, if you hide the truth, then you
will also be hiding your flaws. The people who address their
flaws also happen to become the leaders.

None of us are perfect, and it is important for all of us to
address our own flaws. Maybe you have been spending
hours looking up information but not taking action. When I
first began my journey as an entrepreneur, I was guilty of
making that same mistake. In order for anyone to fix their
flaws, those flaws must first be addressed. Once those
flaws are addressed, solutions can be found. The first part
of *Lead The Stampede* listed some of the flaws that people
face. Those flaws cause oodles of time to slip by to the

point where goals and visions cannot be accomplished simply because no time is allocated to them. This plan, the Productivity Plan, will allow you to identify when you are the most productive, and when you are the least productive. If you are unproductive for a certain week, you need to write down why you were unproductive during that week. If the same problem comes up multiple times, it is a flaw that needs to be addressed and fixed. Being honest with yourself may feel uncomfortable in the beginning, but that honesty will help you in the long run.

It is important to avoid getting discouraged when you have an unproductive week. When you start giving yourself bigger goals, your first week may not be as productive as you want it to be. That is just because you are not used to this new mindset yet. You will not be used to accomplishing your goals in one week instead of one month. Some people throw their plans, hopes, and dreams away because of one lousy week in a quarter, and I do not want you to be one of those people. You have an entire quarter to accomplish what you need to get done. You have enough time, but you don't have too much time. You will have enough time to make up anything you missed for one of the weeks.

During the first week of a quarter, you might give yourself too many tasks that are unrealistic. This will skew how much you get done because you'll overload yourself with too much work. The first week is always going to be the most difficult because it takes some time to adapt and identify standards that are possible but not too easy. Your second quarter is going to be better than your first quarter, and you will get better each time by applying the Productivity Plan. There are going to be some mistakes on the first week, but as you get more experience with the Productivity Plan, you'll make less mistakes and get more work done than ever before.

You are going to feel a bit uncomfortable by giving yourself only a week to accomplish certain goals and phases of big quarterly goals. These phases are the baby steps that will allow you to accomplish your big quarterly goal. The discomfort is essential towards successfully implementing the Productivity Plan because it will create a sense of urgency. When something becomes urgent, we do everything we can to accomplish it. Another way to create urgency is by giving yourself a closer deadline. When you break the quarter into weeks, you will be able to create an environment of urgency in which you will get more accomplished than ever before.

The urgency is going to help you get your goals done, and prioritizing your goals will allow you to decide which goals are the most important. It's great to accomplish your goals, but if you can't utilize those goals, you're not going to get the results you want. Suppose your big goal was to boost visibility for your business' Pinterest account by gaining 10,000 Pinterest followers. If you accomplish the goal of boosting visibility for your business' Pinterest account by gaining 5,000 Pinterest followers, you haven't accomplished the big goal. You have only accomplished it halfway.

The big goals are your priorities. The big goals are those "absolutely-must-get-done" goals. In the example, boosting the visibility for your business' Pinterest account is one of your priorities. Boosting the visibility of your personal Pinterest account is not as important. Once you get the priorities done, you can accomplish the other goals you set for yourself.

This aspect of goal setting changes what it means to set goals for yourself. Creating the list and putting it in a notebook isn't enough. You need to rank your goals based on which ones are the top priorities. If you need to send a client an email before the end of the day, sending that email is the top priority. That goal gets ranked as the top priority. The best way to rank your goals is to use these three factors:

1. The deadline of the goal.
2. The predicted impact accomplishing this goal will have on your business.
3. How much you want to accomplish the goal.

The deadline of the goal is the due date for that goal. Anything due today or tomorrow becomes a top priority. Sending that email to your client becomes the priority because your client expects to receive that email today or tomorrow. It is important to give all of your goals deadlines so you can create the urgency. The urgency you create for yourself will allow you to accomplish your goals faster than ever before. The deadlines you give yourself for all of your goals shouldn't be impossible to reach, but at the same time, you shouldn't be too comfortable. The mentality of a 52 week year will make most people too comfortable. Then, November will come, and an overwhelming sense of discomfort will grasp those people. Creating deadlines for yourself that bring forth some kind of discomfort throughout the year will prevent cramming in all of the work you were supposed to do in the last two months of the year.

Before you set the deadlines for any of your goals, you must finish ranking those goals. The second and third steps will allow you to finish ranking your goals so you can give them their appropriate deadlines. The second factor is the predicted impact that accomplishing the goal will give you. When accomplished, which goals are going to get you the most visibility, the most revenue, and the most traffic? These are referred to as ROI Generating Goals. Your time is valuable, and you need to utilize it effectively. Which of your goals when accomplished will lead to the biggest profit, higher traffic numbers, and the most visibility? Answering these questions will be helpful towards ranking your goals.

You have the list of goals, you wrote down the deadlines, and you predicted the impact accomplishing those goals will have on your business. The third factor will allow you to identify which goals you want to accomplish the most. You might dread one of your goals. The goals you want to work on the most are the ones that you want to accomplish the most. If you want to accomplish something, you will accomplish it with the Productivity Plan. However, if you don't want to accomplish something, you won't try to accomplish that goal. If you focus on the goal that you don't like, you are going to procrastinate and lose time that you could use to accomplish the goals that you want to accomplish.

Do not accomplish a goal primarily because you were told to do so. Where's the logic in that? The goals you accomplish should be the ones related to your mission. While some goals are more enjoyable than others, you need to do the ones that support your mission. Let's say you are a runner who wants to run faster. Running six miles is more painful than running two miles at the same pace. However, running the extra distance allows you to achieve your mission (become a faster runner) in a more effective manner than running the shorter distance.

Before identifying your mission, you need to make sure that you choose a mission that you have a strong passion for. Pretending to enjoy or want something does not work. Pretending does not change the truth. If a high school student does not want to play football, that student's goal should not be to get better at football. If that same student wants to get better at soccer, that should be the student's goal instead.

The mistake many people make with their goals is thinking of the impact but forgetting about choosing goals that match up with their passions. We all enjoy accomplishing our goals, but it takes a lot of time and effort to go from Point A to Point B. There will be some hardships, and it is during those hardships where people ask themselves the question, "Is it worth it?"

Instead of waiting until then to ask yourself that question, I want you to ask yourself that question right now. If you do not like one of your goals, you can remove it from the list before you start. You do not want to figure out that you chose the wrong goal too late. There is no way to regain all of those hours. In order to accomplish any of your goals, you have to **want** to do the work required to accomplish those goals.

The truth about accomplishing goals based on your desire to do them is that it is neither too early nor too late to get started. I have been able to connect with numerous people in their 40s, 50s, and sometimes even older than that who just identified what they want to do. No matter how old or young you are, you can free yourself from the shackles of the status quo and do what you love to do.

By using these three factors, you will be able to find out which of your goals are the priorities. The higher the goal ranks, the more of a priority that goal becomes. The top priorities are the ones that you need to put in the most work for. This will allow you to organize your goals based on the ones that you absolutely need to accomplish and the ones that do not need to be accomplished as much.

The only problem with goal setting is that our minds are quick to trick us. You need to avoid falling into the trap of only setting goals that are in your comfort zone. Sticking with the comfort zone is hardwired into our minds. Goal achievement and leadership among other things require that you take a step out of your comfort zone. Instead of asking yourself what you could do right now, ask yourself how you can do something that you previously thought you could not do (i.e. Go from writing 3,000 words every day to writing 10,000 words every day).

Now that you have ranked your goals and identified the priorities, you need to create a new list of goals. This time, put the priorities on the top of the list and the non-priorities at the bottom of the same list. Once you organize your goals, do not rely on your original list of goals where they are in an unorganized order. Writing out a new list of goals with the priorities on the top and non-priorities on the bottom gives you a better framework which will allow you to accomplish the most important goals on the list. The example below will show you how to implement this technique so you are able to identify your priorities.

| Goals (in a random order) | Priorities (ranked) |
| --- | --- |
| Respond to an email | #1: Continue working on a training course |
| Read niche-related articles on the web | #2: Respond to an email |
| Watch a YouTube video | #3: Read niche-related articles on the web |
| Continue working on a training course | #4: Watch a YouTube video |

Priorities and their rankings are subject to the individual. I prefer to focus on product creation and then respond to emails when I am not creating products. Although it is great to communicate to people through email, this type of communication can eat away at your time. Creating products first ensures that I do something for my business every day before I start responding to emails. After that, I focus on absorbing new knowledge and finally, if I have time left in the day, I may look on YouTube to see what educational and entertaining videos I can find.

After you write your new list of goals, I want you to put that list where you will be able to see it every day. It is very important for you to see that list of goals every day so you know what the priorities are. Every four hours, I want you to ask yourself and *write* this question, "Did I do anything today that allowed me to get closer to living a more fulfilling life and accomplishing my goals?" Asking yourself this question in your mind is not enough. If you did not accomplish, write that down. We do not like to demerit ourselves which is why doing so will give you the motivation you need to do better next time. When you are able to answer yes to that question, write that down too. Being able to write down a list of goals you accomplished and putting checkmarks next to each of those goals will motivate you to go the extra mile and get closer to the front of the stampede. Soon, you will have to write more things on your ever growing list just so you can put checkmarks next to them. Writing the checkmark will allow you to look back at what you have accomplished. The problem with relying on your memory to remember what you have accomplished is that people forget. These people will either forget the goal that got accomplished or the impact it had on their business.

Let's say at one point, whether this would be a past goal or one that you have now, that you wanted to average one sale every day. Later on, if your business becomes well-known, you will get numerous sales every day. When you are getting those numerous sales every day, it is easy to forget the impact of getting one sale a day had on your business. You may be averaging 100 sales every day, and then on one day, you only make 80 sales. The first thing you need to do is find out what went wrong. Maybe the products weren't displayed correctly or it was the day after Christmas when just about everyone gets fewer sales. The second thing you need to do is look back in your notebook and turn to the page that said, "Goal: Make one sale per day," and look at the checkmark.

Looking at the goal with the checkmark is meant to inspire you. You have already accomplished so much by going from only one sale every day to an average of 100 sales every day, and you can accomplish even more great things. This is not meant for you to settle and be happy with going from 100 daily sales to 80 daily sales. By sticking with it, you may end up reaching an average of 101 sales per day which may one day turn into 200 daily sales which may keep on increasing to the point where you are getting over 500 daily sales!

All entrepreneurs come with a story. Seth Godin was denied numerous times by publishers. Mike Michalowicz went in debt after he spent over $1 million. Both are now bestselling authors with multimillion dollar companies. If you follow the plan and stay dedicated towards turning your dreams into realities, you will achieve transformational growths. If you write down all of your goals and checkmark every goal you accomplish, you will be able to look back at Day 1 years later. You will be able to see how far you have gone on your entrepreneurial journey and be grateful for what you have been able to do.

Now that you have written down your priorities, it's time to create the phases of your goal. Phases are the tasks that you need to accomplish so you can reach your goal. Writing "Get 1,000 Twitter followers" is only a goal, and even if that goal is your priority, what happens next? In order to accomplish your goals, you need to create a list of phases for each of your priorities. The phases are bit-sized methods in which you do daily activities that will help you accomplish your goal. Going from 0 followers to 1,000 *real* Twitter followers does not happen overnight. Instead, you will need to gain a certain number of followers every day until you have 1,000 Twitter followers. Then, you raise the bar to 2,000 Twitter followers.

Writing all of the phases for your goals is going to require additional work. This is why you needed to decide which of your goals were the priorities before writing down all of the phases. Only write a complete list of phases for your top priorities. You should write a list of phases for no more than five goals. You can compare this to a two-floor building. The first floor is where you are now and the second floor is where you want to be (in this example, I am talking about individual goals). The first floor and the second floor need to be connected with a staircase. The staircase needs stairs, and those stairs are the phases that will allow you to accomplish your goal. This comparison applies for any of the goals you will accomplish.

Right now, I want you to do a quick activity. It won't take any longer than 15 minutes. I just want you to answer these questions for all of your top priorities:

1. What is your first floor (where you are now)?
2. What is your second floor (where you want to be)?
3. What are the stairs on your staircase (what are the phases that will allow you to accomplish your goal)?

The table on the next page shows these questions in action for someone who wants to go from 500 Twitter followers to 1,000 Twitter followers in 30 days. In this example, there are only three phases. Some goals may have more than three phases, but three phases is the minimum. Anything below that typically indicates a goal that is too easy to reach.

| 1st Floor | Stairs On The Staircase | 2nd Floor |
|---|---|---|
| Where are you now? | Phase #1: Follow targeted people who follow back | Where do you want to be? |
| I have 500 Twitter followers | Phase #2: Make my bio more compelling | I want to have 1,000 Twitter followers in 30 days |
| However, I want to grow my Twitter audience. | Phase #3: Tweet great content and schedule 10 tweets every day. | That means you need to gain about 17 Twitter followers every day |

By answering these questions for your own goals, you will be able to develop a stronger understanding of why you want to accomplish your goal and what accomplishing that goal will do for you. This will give you the motivation you need to accomplish the goals on your list. Writing down your goals will give you some motivation. Organizing those goals and identifying the priorities will give you more motivation. Answering those three questions will give you more motivation as well. In order to be successful with this plan, it needs to be implemented, and it is easy to implement something that you are motivated to accomplish. This part of the plan may be old-school or new-school depending on the way you look at it. At the back of your notebook, I want you to write one motivational quote every day. There are some motivational quotes in this book while others can be searched for via the internet (check out the Top 100 Inspirational Quotes on *Forbes*), apps, and other sources as well. Each time you find a motivational quote that you like, I want you to write it down. Whenever you can, quickly go over the list of motivational quotes you wrote in your notebook. You will be able to remember these motivational quotes. Recalling what you wrote in your notebook will motivate you to complete one of the phases which will allow you to accomplish the ultimate goal.

When you identify the phases, you need to remember that you only have one quarter to accomplish what needs to be done. The people who continue to live with the "365 day year" mentality are going to rush at the end to get everything done. It's not just a mentality, but it is also a trap. No one studies for the end term at the beginning of the year. Most people study for the end term a few days before it takes place. This type of studying and approach to life results in you sacrificing value to get something done on time.

Ideas get rushed and never reach their true potential. The question changes from, "How can I make this better?" to "How can I get this out of the way as soon as possible?" There are many dire consequences that come forth when someone waits at the last minute to start their work. Derek Jeter once said, "You don't just accidentally show up in the World Series." The greatest role models of our time put in years of preparation to attain some of the world's greatest accomplishments.

When you write down a list of phases for each of your goals, you need to make sure it is possible to complete all of those phases before the end of the quarter. Each of the phases of all of your goals should have their own deadlines. If you have one quarter to accomplish a particular goal that has six phases, you should be completing one phase for that particular goal every two weeks. There will be some phases of your goal that you will be able to do within the same week, or even the same day. Some people who strive to lose weight run outside every day and eat differently at the same time. Both running outside and eating differently are phases that can be performed at the same time. Those two phases can even be performed every day for an entire quarter. The amount of phases you will have to juggle at the same time depends on your particular goals.

If you are following through with the plan for the first time, you may be a bit anxious. All of the phases, goals, and priorities are a lot to take in. To a certain extent, implementing the phases, goals, and priorities is going to be uncomfortable. Going from the 365 day year perspective to the 1 quarter perspective is a dramatic change. We are all very resistant to change because we are creatures of habit. However, this change is a good one. You will be able to get more accomplished than ever before by following this plan. The discomfort will eventually turn into a comfortable lifestyle of productivity.

There is just one more thing you have to do with your list of goals. Now that you have addressed the priorities, it's time to address the big quarterly goal. The big quarterly goal is the goal that is going to have the biggest impact on your business, is possible to accomplish in one quarter, and is something you want to do. You should spend a majority of the quarter working on accomplishing your big quarterly goal. This goal can range from getting a new product to finding people from your niche to interview.

The big quarterly goal should take an entire quarter to accomplish. In high school, one of the assignments is a project for the quarter. Out of all of the assignments, students (hopefully) spend the most time working on the project that's due by the end of the quarter. Your big quarterly goal is the project that is due at the end of the quarter. In order to get a good grade, students still have to do the homework that the teacher assigns. The priorities are the homework that the teacher assigns, and the side goals are the extra credit that you do if you have enough time on a test (if the test has extra credit questions). The priorities are essential towards success, and accomplishing the side goals will help out, but accomplishing the big quarterly goal is the enchilada. Combined with other factors and accomplishing the priorities and side goals, accomplishing the big quarterly goal will allow your business to soar to greater heights.

On some occasions, accomplishing your priorities will aid you towards accomplishing your big quarterly goal. If getting twice as many sales is the big quarterly goal, and one of your priorities is to get more blog traffic, your priority is aiding you towards accomplishing the big quarterly goal. For many school students, the big quarterly goal is to end up with a good grade on the report card. Priorities such as doing worksheets and writing essays before their due dates contribute to the quarterly goal. If you have no priorities that line up with your big quarterly goal, you should add one priority that does line up with your big quarterly goal. If you can't think of a priority that lines up with your big quarterly goal, then give yourself enhanced time management as a priority. If you have more time to work on your big quarterly goal, you are going to get a better result when you accomplish your big quarterly goal.

After you address the big quarterly goal, it's time to write the phases that will allow you to accomplish that goal. Since you did the phases for all of your priorities in advance, you will have more time to plan the phases for your big quarterly goal. You have already identified the big quarterly goal as a "must accomplish" goal. All you have to do is give yourself the framework that will allow you to accomplish your big quarterly goal in a step by step action plan.

## Identifying The True And False Priorities

Many people fall into the trap of giving themselves too many priorities. Some priorities are important while other priorities take up space. In order to identify which of your priorities are important and which ones are fluff, you need to think of the big picture. What is the big goal you are trying to accomplish? Are you trying to lose 10 pounds, are you trying to double your income, or are you trying to accomplish something else?

Your priorities should be in line with the big picture. If you are trying to lose 10 pounds, working out more often lines up with your big goal. Working out is a priority that will allow you to accomplish your goal. If you are trying to double your income, asking for referrals is a priority that lines up with your goal.

The priorities that do not line up with any of your goals are unnecessary. When it comes to priorities, people feel as if they need a big list of priorities in order to indicate an increase in progress. All of the priorities will require you to invest your time, and some of the priorities will require you to invest some of your resources into something. You will definitely be investing a lot of time with all of your priorities, but in order to make sure you are getting the best out of your time, you need to make sure all of the priorities line up with your big goal.

If your big goal is to double your income as an author, the priorities should revolve around writing books, marketing the books, talking with customers, and anything similar. Doubling your income as an author does not involve creating a training course about fashion. The training course does have potential to be successful, but creating a training course does not line up with the big picture (doubling your income as an author). Creating the training course would require time on your part, but it is not a good priority because it takes you away from the big picture goal. If you decide you want to change your priorities, I will encourage you to change your priorities after 12 weeks. Brian P. Moran and Michael Lennington wrote an incredible book called *The 12 Week Year* which challenges people to create and implement their goals within a 12 week timeframe. At the beginning of every 12 weeks, write down all of your goals and priorities that you will accomplish in those 12 weeks. After you have gone through the entire 12 weeks, you can give yourself different goals and priorities to accomplish. It is important to avoid changing your goals and priorities while you are investing your time towards accomplishing them.

By being able to identify your priorities and being productive, you will have a distinct advantage in your stampede. You will be able to accomplish more goals at a faster pace and move up in the stampede.

## The Purpose

Why are you working on what you are working on? Why do you want to accomplish the goals you chose to accomplish? The purpose is an essential way to build on the motivation from the vision and direction. The purpose will constantly remind you why you are doing what you are doing. Just reminding yourself of where you want to go and the "why" part will encourage you to accomplish your goals and achieve greatness.

Many people forget about asking themselves why they want to get better or why they want to go from Point A to Point B. Asking yourself the "why" part will allow you to remember why you are working at an uncomfortable rate. For some people, this may be the first time that an uncomfortable rate of work must consistently be performed.

By identifying your purpose, you can also motivate others. You may have had a bad boss and went astray to create your own business. You may have lost your business and decided to create a new one. The great Bill Gates himself did that when Traf-O-Data went out of business. The new business he created ended up being something called Microsoft. You know the rest. Regardless of your current situation, you will always have a purpose. Make sure you know what that purpose is, the "why" part, and tell others about your purpose as well.

People will ask why you started your business. Each time you tell people why you started, you have the opportunity to motivate yourself further. By telling others about your purpose, they will know about it, and you will remind yourself of your purpose. You will remind yourself about why you do what you do, and why you are sticking with it. The more you remind yourself of your purpose, the more motivated and empowered you will be. This kind of motivation and empowerment will result in goal achievement becoming easier to attain.

# The Ability To Take Leaps

The ability to take leaps is important because it allows you to get out of the status quo. In order to lead the stampede, you need to take risks. Some risks will be easier to take than others. By taking risks, you will stand out from the crowd and be an established leader of your niche.

## Fear Stops Us

We all have goals that we want to accomplish. We all have dreams, and we all want them to come true. You might be dreaming of creating a systematized multimillion dollar business. You might be dreaming about creating a business based on what you love instead of working for someone else.

We often stop ourselves short because of the fears of failure and of what others will think. If the business plan doesn't work, and the business collapses, it's back to square one. There are plenty of risks when it comes to accomplishing our dreams. The risk associated with starting a new business is that it may not bring in any revenue. When it comes to adding a new component to your business plan, the fear is that it may not work out and consume too much of your time. Life is risky in itself because not everyone is guaranteed to be successful. We want as many guarantees we can get in life. The problem is that less guarantees are making themselves available. It's not guaranteed that your blog will get a hundred visitors every day. It's not guaranteed that your plan of a systematized business will work. Your startup isn't guaranteed to make millions of dollars.

It is easy to expand on this topic because every goal has a fear factor. In school, athletes like particular sports but do not try out for those sports because they fear getting cut. Taking challenging classes presents some fear because they consume more time, and it gets more difficult to maintain the "A" average.

People fear making a commitment. The person who needs to go to the gym probably won't go. In most cases, if the person decides to go to the gym, that person only goes about once a week. Once a week becomes twice a month, and then the goal is left unaccomplished.

Blogging is an incredible commitment. That's why over 90% of blogs have been abandoned. Most of these people realized the hard way that it doesn't take weeks to get a lot of traffic to your blog. It took some of the most successful bloggers years before they even reached 1,000 daily visitors. Everyone looks at the successful bloggers and they all think it's easy...in the beginning. Most of these people then realize the commitment needed to become a successful blogger and quit. The incredible commitment involved with blogging was a fear factor that stopped them, and unfortunately, it continues to stop others to this day in all types of business.

**Stop Trying To Be Perfect**
It won't work. No leader of any stampede is perfect, no matter what others think. People fear getting judged, and

this stops them from creating great products and following their dreams. Amazon isn't perfect. It took me a month to get one of the items I ordered on Amazon. Facebook gets hacked multiple times every year. One person saw a flaw, told Facebook, and was ignored. That same person ended up posting on Mark Zuckerberg's timeline because of the breach, and it attracted media attention. The iPhone isn't perfect. Some people reported their iPhones would suddenly overheat and melt (that was a while ago. You don't have to worry now, but it did happen).

You may know Hiten Shah and Neil Patel, the co-founders of KISSmetrics. KISSmetrics shows you what happens when someone goes on your blog. Before KISSmetrics, Hiten Shah spent over a million dollars on something that didn't even launch. Shah spent all of that money on his idea that never launched because he was constantly trying to perfect it. Then, he and Neil worked together on KISSmetrics and decided to launch it. KISSmetrics is now a very successful business.

## Think Of Your Idea As A Giant Picture

I want you to imagine your idea as a giant picture. Do you see the big picture, or do you see that small scratch at the corner of the picture. It is very important to avoid looking at that scratch. If there are a lot of scratches, then something has to be done, but if there are only a few scratches, don't worry about them. Scratches indicate imperfection, and every business has them. Not everyone is going to like what you have to offer, but at the same time, there will be people who will buy all of your products. Not everyone likes the Mona Lisa. Then again, there are people who praise the Mona Lisa. Your idea is different from a picture. For ideas, the scratch is only as obvious as you make it out to be. The more you focus on the scratch, the less likely you are to take the leap and launch your idea. There are many people who come up with great ideas. Some of them forget about them while others spend too much time trying to perfect those ideas. The reason so many people are trying to perfect their ideas is because they don't see how great their idea already is; they only see the flaws.

## One Of Eleanor Roosevelt's Quotes
Eleanor Roosevelt was a very credible person who many people admire. Therefore, motivational things that she said must be important and empowering. Here is one of her motivational quotes which you can use to fight against fear.

"Do one thing every day that scares you." --Eleanor Roosevelt

When you take the leap, fear is always going to be involved. There is a risk of failure. The possible failures depend on the leap you plan to take. This failure stops many of us from taking the leap.
I am a firm believer of gradually getting used to change. If someone wanted to go from lifting 5 pound weights to lifting 50 pound weights, we all know that change cannot be made overnight. The person wouldn't be able to even lift

the 50 pound weights off the floor. That dramatic change also risks injury. However, after the person lifts some 10 pound weights, he can move on to the 15 pound weights. Then 15 goes to 20, 20 goes to 25, and 25 eventually goes all the way to the 50 pound weights.

It is important to gradually get used to the change of taking the leap. In order to do this, you need to take one leap-- whether it may be big or small--every day. You'll get better with practice, and taking the leap will become easier. Instead of worrying about failing or getting cut, just take the leap. Fear won't hold you back as much as it used to.

**Taking The Leap May Open A Door That Was Closed**
You may take a leap and look bad. However, taking that leap and looking bad in the beginning may open you up to a new opportunity later on. I got cut from my high school's soccer team, and that was not pretty. Getting cut from the soccer team allowed me to pursue cross country, and that evolved into track. Running every day allowed me to be more committed because if you run 1 month straight, then you know what type of commitment is needed to run every day for the entire year.

**If Zuckerberg Didn't Take The Leap**
Facebook wouldn't exist. If Bill Gates didn't take the leap, Microsoft wouldn't be around. Before Microsoft, Bill Gates co-founded Traf-O-Data which was successful for a few years until its demise. If Steve Jobs didn't take the leap, people would only think of an apple as a fruit, not a

multibillion dollar business. If Jack Dorsey didn't take the leap, we wouldn't be able to understand how special 140 characters are. If Larry Page didn't take the leap, we'd still be going to the libraries...or using Yahoo! more often. If Matthew Mullenweg didn't take the leap, millions of blogs powered by WordPress (such as mine) would not be around. If Ben Silberman and his team didn't take the leap, Pinterest wouldn't exist. If Steven Chen and his team didn't take the leap, YouTube wouldn't exist. If Pierre Omidyar didn't take the leap, people wouldn't be able to sell their left over products on eBay. If Jeff Bezos didn't take the leap, people would refer to Amazon as a river in South America. If Elon Musk and his team did not take the leap with Tesla, we would only talk about electric cars as if they were a fantasy.

There are so many things that could have happened if these people did not take their respective leaps. All of these people faced challenging tasks that they didn't give up on. Taking the leap does involve taking risks. Amazon could have failed. Facebook could have been abandoned. Google could have gotten no visitors. Pinterest could have been ignored since Facebook and Twitter were already powerful social networks.

When you take the leap, you open yourself to potential rewards. You can end up with the next Facebook. You can end up with the next Amazon. You can end up with something incredible. You may even stumble the first time like Bill Gates did and then create a multibillion dollar business. However, the only way to get that far is by taking the leap.

## What's The Best Case Scenario?

It's a shame that we always think of the worst case scenario. The average person might be thinking this: "The worst that can happen is that my business collapses, my product doesn't sell, and all of the time and energy that I committed to this idea for months were wasted. If that happens, I'll have to start all over again and then think of another worst case scenario."

That's the typical worst case scenario syndrome, and many people think of it too often. Did you know that the more we think about things, the more likely they are to happen? If you keep on thinking about that worst case scenario, it is going to happen, so stop thinking about it! If you constantly think of the worst case scenario, you will never be able to take the leap and possibly see your idea thrive. Many people are haunted by the illusions of failure that they give themselves. The unfortunate fate for these people is that they look back at their lives and regret what they were not able to accomplish. Then, these people finally prepare to take the leap, but then they hear that whisper, "What if you don't make it?"

The reason why people live in regret is because they let all of the worst case scenarios prevent them from making better decisions. Instead of thinking of the worst case scenario, I want you to think of the best case scenario. Your business will thrive, your leap will be huge, you will make it to the other side and go far beyond! Your product will sell, you will get partners for your next event, people will be lining up for your autograph, and more! Those are all of the wonderful things that can happen after you take the leap. That's the best case scenario.

When you think of your best case scenario, you will be more motivated to continue what you started. Instead of focusing on the negative energy, you will focus on the vision of a bright future and countless possibilities. When you see a bright future, you will take more leaps to reach that vision. You won't stop short when you think of your best case scenario. In fact, you'll have to come up with a scenario that is better than your best.

## Safe Isn't Safe

If you do not take the leap, you will be safe. At least, that's what the status quo wants you to think. The problem is that there are thousands of people who are not taking the leap. The problem with not taking the leap is that your products, services, and business blend in with thousands or even millions of other people.

If you are safe, then you are not safe at all. You are only putting yourself in danger. In order to make people remember who you are, you have to give them a good reason to remember you. We know what WalMart is because they have the lowest prices that are different from the competition. We know what Apple is because they sell quality products that are different. Taking the leap involves being different from the competition in as many ways as you can. The more different from the competition you are, the more people will remember you. If you are afraid of taking the leap because it's dangerous, it is important to know that you are in some kind of danger now. You are in the danger of stagnancy. Even the leading competitors can get defeated because other startups are willing to take more leaps. Those leaps are also bigger than the competitors' leaps. Then, the startup ends up becoming the leaders.

## The Lesson In Green Eggs And Ham

You may be hesitant to take the leap. There are going to be risks associated with the leap you take. Some people will have more risks to face than others. However, it is important to take the leap because you will be better off. This isn't a gamble. If you take the leap and mess up, you have something to learn from. After taking the leap many times, you will eventually make it, and making it on the other side allows you to tap into your potential.

I know this is a very dramatic transition for many people, but you need to take impactful and numerous leaps. In the book *Green Eggs And Ham* by Dr. Seuss, the main character, Sam, does not like green eggs and ham. He won't eat them on a train, in the rain, in a house, or with a mouse (there are a lot of other ones in the book). However, Sam eventually tries the green eggs and ham. Once he finally *tries* the green eggs and ham, he likes them. He says he will eat them on a train, in the rain, in a house, and with a mouse.

Learning and doing are two different things. If someone learns everything there is to know about coding but that person becomes a dentist, a small percentage of that person's knowledge about coding (if any at all) gets used as a dentist.

Sam didn't like green eggs and ham. Sam did not want to take the leap and see if the green eggs and ham were good or not. He had to be persuaded for a long time until he finally decided to give the green eggs and ham a try. After taking the leap, Sam realizes that green eggs and ham are better than sliced bread. That's a successful leap. If you take enough leaps, you will become successful at what you do and lead your stampede. You must constantly try new ideas and never become stagnant.

**We Have More Time Than We Think We Realize**
One of the reasons why people don't take the leap is because taking the leap requires a lot of time on your part. Going from sending 5 tweets a day to 20 tweets a day requires more time and effort. Going from writing 500 words every day to writing 1,000 words every day requires twice the amount of time. Going from no business to becoming an entrepreneur requires more time as well.

There is no shortcut when it comes to the amount of time it will take for your business to develop. There are only 24 hours in a day. You are going to be sleeping during some of those hours, eating for other hours, and doing other things for some of those hours as well. Most people see their time

getting cut down from 24 hours to only 10-15 minutes that they can use to work on their business and take the leap. The reason 24 hours got chopped down to only 10-15 minutes of working on a goal is because most people spend too much time procrastinating. Some people watch their favorite TV shows for countless hours. Other people surf the web. There are more distractions than ever in today's world. Those distractions cut the 24 hours into 10-15 minutes. Believe it or not, if you took out some of those distractions, you could probably work on preparing to take the leap for at least an hour or two every day.
That's a lot of extra time. There are no special exceptions to the rule. Everyone has the ability to find an hour every day to work on taking their own leap whether the leap involves a business or conquering a fear. The problem is that many people accept the fact that they have little time to work on accomplishing their goals but don't do anything about it. When you stop finding ways to give yourself more time, you will be less likely to take the type of daring leaps that lead to big rewards. If you find more time to work on accomplishing a goal, you will also get closer to taking the leap.

**You Do Not Have To Start Out As The Best**
We all want to be #1 at something. However, there are many people competing for that #1 slot. Some people are spending more time perfecting their ideas and less time implementing them. In order to succeed, you have to realize that you won't start out as the best.

Doing great work and forgetting the rest has become very popular advice to follow. It's also good advice to follow. You don't have to have 100,000 followers before you launch your product. You don't have to have a bestselling product before you come out with your next product. You don't have to be perfect or the best before you start. Everyone stumbles at a given point in time. Michael Jordan got cut from the high school basketball team, but that didn't stop him from being the best in NBA history. The only way to become the best is with practice. The baseball players got where they are today by practicing for a long time. Becoming the best is some of the motivation, but making the big leagues and being able to be a part of the sport is another strong motivational tool.

Like baseball players, you don't have to be perfect the first time you step on the diamond. Every baseball player struck out. Ted Williams struck out. Babe Ruth struck out. Derek Jeter has struck out a bunch of times as well. All three of these baseball players are incredible. I could name countless other players who are incredible, but that would take too long. The bottom line is that they have all struck out. They have struck out in the 9th inning when their teams counted on them the most. Now let's talk about pitchers. All pitchers lost games or blew save opportunities. You don't have to be the #1 person in order to be successful. People who are focusing on being the best should instead focus on actually practicing and doing the work. If you focus on practicing and doing the work, you will take bigger leaps which will allow you to become more successful in the process.

## Take Action Now, Not Later

The best way to take the leap is to take it as soon as possible. Too many people are thinking about taking the leap which results in few people *actually* taking it. Greatness may be on the other side, but without a leap, you don't get to find out what was on the other side. You don't get to the other side where greatness may be waiting for you. That gruesome word, "failure" comes into play right about now. That word makes more people dwell and prolong the leap.

The thought of failing makes an activity go from favorable to a problematic situation. This is where people think of the worst case scenario instead of the best case scenario. People can dwell on the leap they want to take for days, weeks, months, or even years. The more dwelling a person does, the less time that person gets to take action. The only way to take the leap is to take action. It isn't bad to feel unprepared when you take the leap.

## When You Only Take One Leap

There have been people and companies who only take one leap. The leap they took gave them an edge on the competition, but when a person or company stops taking leaps, that edge gets lost. More people and companies will take more leaps in order to catch up to the top competitor. Soon, that person or company who only took one leap to get ahead of everyone else has to take more leaps in order to catch up to everyone else.

Taking only one leap, being risky only once, accomplishing something incredible only once, is not going to work anymore. Amazon continues taking leaps to this day, and having drones deliver goods is just one of the many recent leaps they have taken. We are in a world now where more people are going to take leaps. That means more people are going to mess up, but it also means more people are going to succeed. The best part about a bad leap is that by taking enough bad leaps, you will be able to take a strong leap that propels you past numerous competitors that never thought you could surpass.

In order to keep what you got from taking your first leap, you need to frequently take other leaps as well. If taking the leap involves changing one of your habits, you are going to have to take more leaps in order for those changes to stick. If you want to be able to dedicate 30 extra minutes to work on your business, you need to carve out time to make that happen. That's the first leap. The second leap would be to watch less TV. The third leap would be to stop surfing the internet. After taking these leaps, you may end up taking leaps that have strong impacts on your business and yourself.

One leap leads right into the next. When you go through a sequence of leaps, each leap becomes easier than the last. It is up to you to take as many leaps as you can so you can accomplish more of your goals in your lifetime.

## Another Approach To Taking The Leap

One way to take the leap is just to take one giant leap all together to get from where you are to where you want to be. In comparison, it would be jumping from one side of a cliff to the other side. That leap may seem too challenging or too risky for some people. Another way to take the leap is with stepping stones. I don't know how stepping stones could go from one side of a real cliff to the other, but I think you get the idea. If you use multiple stepping stones to get to the other side of the cliff, you are still taking a big leap. It takes longer for you to get to the other side since you are taking smaller leaps, but the quantity of leaps will eventually give you the desired result--the big, impactful leap. Once you get used to using the stepping stones, I want you to take the bigger leaps so you can accomplish more and learn from your mistakes in a shorter amount of time.

## The Problem With Waiting For Later

Almost every time, later never gets done. If you do not want to take the leap now, you won't want to take the leap later. Later halts progress like a fortress stops an army. The longer you wait to take the leap, the longer it will take for you to unlock your potential. In order to successfully take leap after leap, you must be a NOW-Person. There is no way around it, so don't go looking for another route. The more things you do now, the more you will be able to accomplish later on.

## Taking The Leap Is More Important Than Ever

We have more resources than ever before that can help us take more leaps. We are able to communicate and obtain information faster than any other civilization of any other time period. We have what we need to take our own leaps. In fact, we have more than what we need. The problem is that there are millions of people using the same resources in the same way to produce the same results. When millions of people are doing the same thing, it's difficult to decide who to go with.

It has become dramatically easier to create your own business now than a few years ago. It is easier to acquire a new skill because it seems as if there's a YouTube video or blog post for everything. More people are taking advantage of all of these new opportunities. Publishing a book used to take forever. Now authors have the option to self-publish their books. Creating DVDs and CDs is also a lot easier. More things are being done electronically, and the rules have changed. More rules will continue to change. 3D printing changed the rules because merchandise is now a lot easier to create and replicate. We can only wonder which rules will change next. Maybe it will get easier to do your own movie and get it in Cinema. In order to change the rules of your niche, you need to be willing to take a leap.

Another reason why taking the leap is so important is because it allows you to stand out. Let's say you were at a giant business expo with 10,000 people. Everyone at the event is wearing a blazer. Chances are you are going to skip over all of the people in the black blazers because there are so many black blazers. However, if you see someone wearing a purple blazer, you'll look at that person for awhile. The person in the purple blazer stands out.

In order to stand out, you have to be different from everyone else. You don't have to wear a purple blazer in order to be different. Being different simply means doing the things that your competitors wouldn't even dream of doing. Taking more leaps will allow you to further differentiate yourself from the competition. By getting enough practice at taking big leaps, you will be able to take *the leap* that will catapult you to success.

## Leap: Apple Broke Its iPhone Rule

Apple is the world's top brand, and their devices are remarkable. One of their popular devices is the iPhone. Apple has been consistently releasing 1 iPhone after the other, and all of those iPhones were sold a year apart. This remained constant for awhile. Then, Apple decided to change its rule. Instead of selling one iPhone, Apple decided to sell two iPhones at the same time. Many believed that Apple was making a mistake. People thought that the two iPhones would be competing for sales, and as a result, less sales would be made.

The iPhone 5C and iPhone 5S are different in a variety of ways. The 5C has more colors to choose from, but the 5S has a better camera. The 5C has better prices, but the 5S comes with more quality. There are many reasons to go with the 5C, but there are also many reasons to go with the 5S. A competition with one winner between the two devices seemed inevitable.

As a result of that big leap, Apple broke its sales record (again). For the first *weekend,* Apple's 5C and 5S iPhones made 9 million sales. Apple did not fall apart or see a slight decline in sales. Instead, Apple broke another one of its records for iPhone sales. Even the big brands are taking leaps in order to improve upon what they already have. There are no limits to what any brand can accomplish, and in order to surpass expectation after expectation, brands have to take the leap.

## Which Rules Are Worth Breaking?

I recently had the honor of winning the Rule Breaker Award with my brother for teaching teens at a university before attending one. We taught the teens in our Teenager Entrepreneur Bootcamp how to become successful before they graduate college (or high school for that matter). While small businesses are breaking rules to make themselves stand out, even the large brands like Apple are breaking the rules. Apple broke one of it's rules by coming out with two iPhones at the same time. Not all rules are worth keeping, and by breaking some of the established rules of your niche, you will be taking the leap. There are some rules that aren't worth breaking. If someone breaks the rule of practicing and showing up, that person's ideas are going to break too.

Not all rules are good ones, and some rules can be improved. However, we have been taught to obey all of the rules we are given. Don't be afraid to break the rules. In fact, be a rule breaker because by breaking the rules, you'll stand out from the competition. By breaking a rule you have followed for your business, you could make record breaking sales just like Apple did (again).

## How Many Choices Are You Giving Your Clients?

For a few years in a row, Apple released one iPhone each year. For all of those years, Apple would only give its customers one option, and sales would grow every year. In 2013, Apple did something different by giving people two choices between the iPhone 5C and 5S. The iPhone 5C was primarily a beginner's iPhone while the 5S as some people say is "as perfect as you're going to get."

You can take the leap in your own business by giving your clients more choices. You can give them the ability to choose from low-priced products, high-priced products, and the products in between. Try publishing two books this year instead of one and see where that gets you. When Apple offered an extra choice, they got record breaking sales. I'm sure there are people right now saying, "Well, they're Apple. They're just that good."

However, Apple got twice the media coverage than it normally got for its other iPhones. The main reason this happened is because some people reviewed the iPhone 5C, others reviewed the iPhone 5S, and others reviewed both of the smartphones. Some consumers got confused and wondered if the new iPhone was called the 5C or the 5S. Much to their amazement, two iPhones were being sold at the same time. They told their friends about it, and the message got out. Sure enough, more people than ever were ready to click that "Buy now" button the minute Apple put those iPhones up for sale. It's not just because "they're Apple" that they were able to pull this off. Offering an additional option allowed them to reap the rewards.

When you make the decision to give your consumers more choices, make sure the choices don't take up too much of your time to execute. If you're offering two extra options that constantly involve hours of your time every day, that won't work. If you're offering two extra products that are systematized, you'll be able to save more time and see more results come in.

## The Responsibility Of The Leap

If you take the leap, you are responsible for what happens; whether it is a success or failure. Many people start to think more about their responsibility halfway through their leap. Some of these people mess up the leap by thinking of all of their responsibilities. It's like having the weight of the world on your shoulders (or something like that).

In order to take a leap of any kind, you are responsible for starting. A horse can be led to water, but it is up to the horse to do the smart thing which is to drink the water (unless that water is poisonous). Start now so you won't have to worry about it later.

## What Collapse?

There are going to be people who don't get the desired results when they take the leap. Not everyone gets the desired results the first time. Failure is not final. There are a lot of bestselling authors who got denied by a lot of book publishers. They didn't stop. Now those same authors are writing book after book; bestseller after bestseller.

If you do not take the right leap, and you end up in a bad position, you can take the leap again. There is no limit to the number of leaps you can take. The more times you fail, the closer you are getting to success. Babe Ruth, one of the best baseball players in history said, "Every strike brings me closer to my next home run."

Swinging and missing at the plate do not indicate failure, and neither do strikeouts. Those mistakes won't define a person's career because there will always be room for success. No matter where you are or what you have, you have the ability to succeed.

## Kelsey Shane's Leap

Therapists are constantly deciding whether "to niche or not to niche." The risk with joining a specific niche within therapy is that a therapist could lose out on hundreds of customers. However, by narrowing down their number of customers, therapists who join a specific niche within therapy represent themselves as one of the few options available for some people.
When the question came up, Kelsey Shane decided to become a part of a specific niche within therapy. Kelsey Shane works with LGBTQ and self-harm clients. Although it takes most therapists 2 years to build a full-time, sustainable practice, Kelsey was able to build a full-time, sustainable practice in only 4 months. Kelsey said that her

quick success was a combination of factors. One of her biggest factors was her networking. Kelsey did some out of the box networking such as meeting with lawyers who work with similar clients that Kelsey works with. Kelsey has made several connections and has been able to use them as valuable resources to spread the word about her. Kelsey's clients refer their friends over to her because the clients enjoy her help.

Kelsey took a big leap by joining a specific niche in therapy. While losing access to hundreds of potential customers, Kelsey was able to connect with the people who needed her specific expertise. Self-harm and LGBTQ people don't just look for any therapist. These people look for a therapist who is in the self-harm and LGBTQ niches. By taking the leap, Kelsey was able to build a full-time, sustainable practice 8 times faster than the average therapist.

**Preparing To Take The Leap: Twitter Files For IPO**

"Twitter files for IPO" was the headline for the social network's big move. We were all amazed when we first heard about Twitter filing for IPO. Twitter did a good job preparing for the IPO which was a big leap. The first thing Twitter did was announce it was filing for IPO on it's official account. The tweet got retweeted over 10,000 times.

Twitter's tweet could have been enough preparation for that leap. However, Twitter wanted to look nice and polished for the investors. Twitter killed off many of its spam accounts so it could provide advertisers with realistic user numbers.

Twitter made sure it was well prepared to take the leap. It is important to note that plenty of spam accounts were killed off quickly after Twitter made it's announcement. Successful entrepreneurs have the habit of releasing something before they feel absolutely ready. Twitter was prepared for their IPO, but they weren't perfectly prepared. Some changes were still being made after Twitter made the announcement. In fact, some changes are being made on Twitter to this day.

## Don't Rush The Leap

Some people wanted Twitter stocks as soon as they could get them, but some people didn't pay attention to a crucial detail. When you take your leap, it's very important for you to look at the crucial details. Those crucial details help out towards taking an incredible leap. Anyway, the people who didn't do their homework ended up getting TWTRQ stocks. The only problem is that there's no "Q" in Twitter.

TWTRQ stocks weren't Twitter stocks then, and they aren't Twitter stocks now. Twitter decided to use TWTR for it's stock name. There were a lot of people who didn't see the "Q" at the end. The TWTRQ stock went up 1,400% just because it looked like TWTR.

Taking the leap, not rushing the leap, taking action, and implementing your ideas are important towards taking the leap. However, it's just as important to create something that provides value, and make sure your information is accurate. Taking the leap is important, but taking the leaps that matter is just as important.

## Go For Your Dreams

There is no limit to how much we can dream. When we accomplish one of our dreams, we can dream about ourselves accomplishing something even greater in that area. If a track runner runs a certain time, that runner's next big dream is to run a better time. That athlete will develop into a very good one as long as that athlete keeps on dreaming of bigger goals and continues to chase after them. When you take the leap, you need to think about where you are going. Are you going somewhere you want to be, or are you going somewhere to get more money, make the college application look a little better, or just for bragging rights? Those aren't good reasons to take the leap.

The best leaps result when you go for your dreams. Your dreams are real, and the desire to achieve your dreams is real as well. We all have that dream of what we want to be. Maybe you dreamed of becoming a baseball player. Maybe you dreamed of coming up with the next Facebook. Maybe you are still dreaming of becoming those things. You have dreamed of accomplishing many feats, and now is the perfect time for you to take action.

Dreaming big allows you to conquer a powerful foe: limitation. People are limiting their dreams to what seems to be reachable. When I say reachable, I am referring to something that can be reached without putting in all of the work and effort you could be putting in. When you go for what others perceive as the unreachable, and you put in the work and effort, the "unreachable" will get obtained. The lower you set the bar, the lower you go. Likewise, the higher you set the bar, the higher you will go.

In fact, taking the leap and knowing where you want to land is a great starting point towards great achievement. The dream has been manifested in your mind for so long, and now you have the ability to take steps of action in order to implement that dream and turn it into a reality. You want to be the leader of the right stampede, the one that you want to be a part of. Not only will you be very motivated when you take this kind of leap, but you will also want to take more leaps as well. The more leaps you take, the closer you are to becoming very successful at what you do. When you become successful, taking more leaps may allow you to thrive even more.

Our dreams allow us to see ourselves in a fantasy world that we wish was real. However, turning that fantasy into the real world around you is not as difficult as it seems.

There are plenty of dreamers who turned their dreams into things that we know very well. Amazon started out as a dream. Apple started out as a dream. Every social network and successful business started out as a dream.

## Dare To Fail (And Then Succeed)

When you take a lot of leaps, there are going to be some roadblocks. There are going to be times when you make mistakes, and you don't get the results you were expecting. The "A" student doesn't get A's on all of the tests. The "A" students does well on many of the tests, but some of those tests will have bad scores.

Failure is going to happen. In nearly all cases, the number of failures will be greater than the number of successes. It's important to dare to fail. No matter what you do, daring to fail will allow you to become successful in the long run. Not everyone makes the cut for a college, a sports team, or a mastermind group. However, it is better to fail than it is to not try at all and constantly wonder what would have happened if you tried.

Even the most successful people in society failed many times before they become successful. Before Microsoft, Bill Gates co-founded Traf-O-Data which went out of business a few years later. However, the persistent people will eventually succeed. When these people succeed, they aren't "just making it." In fact, these people only started to thrive when they respectively came up with and implemented powerful ideas.

There's no escape from failure. Failure can mean a variety of things for different individuals. To some people, failure is the end of the world. To others, failures are stepping stones to success. It is better to see failures as stepping stones than barriers that prevent us from moving forward. The response to failure is going to be tested again and again. The results we strive for will not always be the ones we want. There will be stumbles and miscues. We will all face failures. It is how we respond to these failures that determines how successful we become down the road.

## The Only Way To Find Out What The Results Of The Leap Would Be Is To Take The Leap

There is no crystal ball that will tell us whether our leaps are good or not. No one from the future is going to magically appear and let you know whether your leap is a good one or not. This makes people reluctant towards taking leaps. Success is not certain, and failure is quite possible. In fact, failure is common even amongst the best of us.

The thought of failure scares many people. The fear of failure makes success seem impossible. You will never know how effective your leap is unless you take the leap, or as people say, "Walk the walk and talk the talk." Your leap has the potential to catapult you towards great success, or your leap can have a bad result.

Leaders are constantly taking new leaps. Some of those leaps result in multibillion dollar businesses. Other leaps result in failures that when accumulated over time can lead to success. Regardless of a leap's result, leaders ultimately learn from their mistakes with each leap they take. By learning from their mistakes and taking leap after leap, leaders eventually take the leaps that transform their business and allow them to lead the stampede.

Taking the leap may be the difference between making the same amount of sales you are making now and 10 times as many sales. Whether you get 100 extra sales or 100,000 extra sales, those extra sales are going to have a positive impact on your business. Not all leaps are going to work, but when you take the right leap, you will know that it was the right leap to take.

Instead of thinking of what your leap can do for your business, take that leap. Thinking about the results will not allow those results to come. In order to get the results you want, you need to take action. The only way you will find out whether your leap is going to be successful is by taking the leap in the first place.

## The Greatest Enemy Of Success Is Fear

Fear holds us back from achieving our dreams. We have the ability to literally astound ourselves, but fear prevents many people from doing that. In order to take leaps, your faith in yourself and your idea need to overcome your fear. Fear prevents the good ideas from coming earlier. Success has the power to triumph against fear, and it comes as a result of starting and persevering until it becomes a reality.

## Why We Become Fearful

Since fear is the greatest enemy of success, it is important to know why we become fearful. The reason we become fearful is because we don't know what is going to happen. There is a risk factor, and that uncertainty scares people. Things could go horribly wrong. Thinking of the negative aspect will let the fear creep in. Thinking of everything that could go right and giving your idea a try will push fear away.

The leaders of the stampede pushed their fear away when they tried their ideas. I am sure that every leader had a moment of fear that something would not work. Not only am I sure that has happened, but I am also certain that it has happened to everyone. Instead of letting the fear consume them, the leaders decided to push that fear into the back of their minds so they could focus on turning their idea into thriving businesses, products, and services. By focusing on

107

turning their ideas into realities, the leaders were able to do just that.

Fear will try to stop us from accomplishing many of our goals. The only way fear will stop an individual from accomplishing their goals is if they give fear permission to do so. Don't give fear the permission to stop you from accomplishing your goals. Don't think about the goal for too long because then it won't happen. Start the goal and take action as soon as possible so fear becomes an afterthought.

# Creativity

Leaders do not simply do what everyone else does. Anyone can do that. Instead, leaders are different. They experiment with different choices in order to get the best result. Some results are good while others are bad, but from each experiment, the leaders learn different techniques that eventually allow them to get incredible results. The more creative you are, the more likely you are to come up with a small innovation that has a big impact on the world. Creativity is essential towards coming up with remarkable ideas that are destined for success. In this part of *Lead The Stampede*, I will provide numerous true stories about how entrepreneurs were able to use their creativity to bring forth small innovations and lead their stampedes. My goal for this part of *Lead The Stampede* is to allow you to realize that being creative and coming up with the small innovation is not as challenging as many people think.

## The Experts And Creativity

Not every 'expert' is an expert, and no expert knows every answer to every question. The experts are not the ultimatums of the world. If you don't agree with what an expert is saying, you don't have to do what the expert says. I don't agree with the experts who say you have to use online advertisements to increase traffic. Experts are recommending Google AdWords to get out there, but I don't agree with those experts.

Just because I disagree with these experts does not necessarily make them wrong. I just prefer to take another approach towards getting the same result. Instead of using AdWords, I use my guest posts on other blogs as my version of an advertisement. Instead of finding me on Google because of AdWords, people find me on Google because I guest blog on various blogs related to my niche. People know who I am on the web because I decided to write numerous guest posts on a popular blog and grew my social media audience, not because I decided to pay $0.10 or so per click.

Are all experts wrong? I would say not. It just depends on what your objectives are and how you want to reach those objectives. Some people will agree with me while others will disagree with me. Some people will believe that AdWords is the way to get more blog traffic while others will agree that guest blogging is the better option.

It seems as if more people than ever are calling themselves experts at something. The word expert is an overused one. If you have a big audience of people who appreciate the knowledge you have to offer, and you have the credibility to go along with it, then you are an expert. Not everyone will see you as an expert, but as long as there is a big audience of people who are being empowered by your expertise, you will be recognized as an expert in your niche.

One of the purposes of experts is for them to say what worked for *them.* It is entirely possible to use different methods to achieve the same goal. Some people are able to get more book sales because they have big social media audiences while others get more book sales with a big email list. Both of those options are methods that people are using to reach the same goal. Here's where the creativity comes in. Most people are doing exactly what their competitors are doing. Every blogger has the goal of building their email list, and every social media expert has the goal of making their audience larger than it already is. In some cases, all you have to do is one thing differently that works, and then you have a winning formula. You can be creative and find a way to achieve the same goal better than the experts or getting there faster by utilizing different methods.

**When I First Saw Origami**

I will never forget when I saw origami in action for the first time. When I first saw it, I was very young and never thought paper could be used to create swans, frogs, dog faces, praying mantises, fish and more. I saw origami as a very creative way to use something as ordinary as paper to create objects that look incredible.

I decided to practice creating origami. When I created origami, I quickly became good at it. Looking back, I remember what it felt like to first see origami. To this day, I have a zip lock bag with about 25 origami creations. Some were made by me and others were bought. Origami represents a different way to use paper. People use paper to draw figures, write essays, take tests, and create paper airplanes. Sure, there are other uses for paper, but the thought of creating origami is something that less people think of. That's what makes origami creation different.

When most people think of utilizing paper, they think of taking a test, drawing an object, or making a paper airplane. There are not as many people who would create an origami figure with that paper. In most parts of the world, these people, the origami creators, are hard to find. The people leading their stampedes are the ones who decided to create origami with their paper. They are the rare, hard to find people in their niche that do something that most of the other people would not think of. Be the origami creator of your niche and be different (but in a good way).

**Be Remarkable**

There are numerous individuals and businesses that strive to stand out from the crowd and lead the stampede. Being remarkable is a staple towards standing out from the crowd. If you want to be remarkable, people need to have a reason to tell their friends about your business. If there are two sellers who sell the same exact products, offer the same exact advice, and are in the same exact niche, people are not going to tell their friends about those two sellers. Those sellers are not remarkable. They are the norm. If you want to be talked about, you need to be different from those two sellers and the other ones as well. You don't have to ride around in a clown car and honk a horn as you give advice to be different (although that would be very interesting). You need to be remarkable by making the small changes.

## Is Being Remarkable Challenging

There are so many ways to become remarkable. You can be remarkable for low prices, quality products, quality service, writing more than anyone else, selling more than anyone else, how you start or end your YouTube videos, and the list keeps on going. There are an unlimited amount of ways to become remarkable, but the problem is that many people do not make a choice.

The amount of options overwhelms many people. When people try to become remarkable, the leaps they have to take look too scary. Risk and the fear of failure overwhelm people. There are many factors that overwhelm people before they try to become remarkable.

Once you decide to try to become remarkable, and you identify how you want to be remarkable, you need to pursue the biggest challenge of them all: starting the journey. The second biggest challenge is identifying how you want to be remarkable. If you get through those two big challenges, you will discover that being remarkable is not as challenging as many people think.

While finding a new niche will allow you to be remarkable, finding a new niche is not necessarily the only or the best way to be remarkable. Social media was around before Mark Zuckerberg and Jack Dorsey founded Facebook and Twitter respectively. However, neither Zuckerberg nor Dorsey found a new niche. MySpace was around before Facebook and Twitter, and Friendster was around before all three of those social networks. Zuckerberg and Dorsey just decided to make their social networks different. Facebook and Twitter have their similarities and differences. When you think of differences, the first thing that probably comes to mind is Twitter's 140 character limit. Facebook and Twitter are different from each other which is why both of them are remarkable even though they are both social networks.

Two identical social networks are not going to be remarkable. The social network that was the first one around is going to be remarkable while the second one is just a copy. If someone creates a social network identical to Twitter, people would not be rushing over to that social network. If you create a product or service identical to one being offered, you are not being remarkable. Luckily, there are many ways to be remarkable without copying someone else. Being remarkable can be as challenging to finding a new niche to as simple as wearing a green blazer. It is how you use the attention you get that will ultimately decide what results you attain from being remarkable. Remarkable is not an impossibility that is granted to a select few. Everyone has the ability to become remarkable. By being remarkable, people will talk about your business and services. People will recommend you to their friends.

## The Koumpounophobia Factor

Has anyone noticed that Mac computers have less buttons than the average computer. The power button for a Mac computer is all the way in the corner, and it often goes unnoticed. There are more buttons on other computers, and those buttons are also easier to see than the power button all the way at the corner on a Mac.

What about the iPhone. I'm sure more people noticed that the iPhone just has the square button at the center. There are only a few other buttons on an iPhone compared to Androids and other smartphones that have numerous buttons. Every other kind of popular smartphone has more buttons than the iPhone.

Now let's take a look at Steve Jobs, the visionary who turned Apple from near bankruptcy to a multibillion dollar business. He did many presentations for his products. The crowds would applaud as he would go over the features of the next Apple product. If you look at a picture of Steve Jobs presenting, you will notice something. Steve Jobs never wore a shirt with buttons.

This is a detail that commonly goes unnoticed. Now you are probably wondering why Jobs never wore a buttoned shirt of any kind. That's because Steve Jobs had koumpounophobia which is the fear of buttons. Jobs was able to turn this fear of buttons into a big advantage that would make Apple's products unique.

That's why the power button of a Mac is all the way on the right corner. That's why the mouse that connects to the Mac does not have any buttons. All you need to do is push down on the mouse and move it around, but without the buttons. That's why the iPhone only has that one button down at the bottom and then some smaller buttons on the top of the iPhone while other phones have dozens of buttons. If the iPhone had dozens of buttons, Steve Jobs would have been afraid of his own creation. Changing your product so it does not conflict with one of your fears is a creative way to potentially create a better product. Fears can be used as strengths that allow you to transform your products and services. Steve Jobs' fear of buttons was one of the factors that allowed Apple products to stand out from the competition which also allowed Apple to go all the way from the back of the stampede to the front.

**Breaking The Rule**
We have always been taught that rules were made to be followed. There are classroom rules, rules of conduct, and rules at baseball stadiums. Some of the entrepreneurial rules are made to be followed, but many of the other rules are made to be broken (as long as it's legal).

There are many examples of how entrepreneurs broke the rules of their niche to go into an uncontested area of their niche. These entrepreneurs were able to take an alternate path from the competition and end up in the front of the stampede. The competitors try to take the path, but the first person who took the path already has the head start. The competitors were trying to catch up to someone in a marathon who had a 5 mile start. Catching up is unlikely, but quite possible.

Although many people focus on the bad consequences, there are also good consequences that come from breaking the rules. The only way to know what the result will be is by giving it a try. Don't be afraid of breaking the rules of your niche. Keep on experimenting, and then identify which rule, when broken, will lead to the greatest success. Many entrepreneurs have broken the traditional rules, and other entrepreneurs are going to break other rules in the future.

### Karen R. Koenig Goes Against The Conventional Methods Of Dieting For Long-Term Weight Loss

Karen R. Koenig is a distinguished "normal" eating guru, psychotherapist, a worldwide eating coach, and an international author of five books on eating and weight loss. As a psychotherapist in private practice with an MSW, Karen brands herself as an expert in the psychology of eating--the how and the why instead of the what. Karen identifies the unexamined issues people need to explore and resolve in order to become normal eaters. Instead of focusing on weight, Karen focuses on the psychological and emotional reasons that people eat under stress and when they are distressed.

Karen knew the conventional methods of dieting were based on worn out perspectives, and as a dieter herself,

Karen got tired of obsessing about food and weight. After reading books such as Susan Orbach's *Fat Is A Feminist Issue*, Karen stopped restricting food and eventually became a normal eater. Karen has written six books about eating and weight such as *Starting Monday* and *The Rules of "Normal" Eating.* as well as her own blog, www.karenrkoenig.com. Karen has differentiated herself from the competition and continues to share her message and expertise with others.

## Kevin Stone's Creativity Allows Him To Create Remarkable Products And Startups

In addition to being a doctor who helps professional, amateur, and every day patients with knee, ankle, and shoulder injuries at Stone Clinic in San Francisco and conducting research at The Stone Research Center, Kevin Stone finds the time to invent products and create companies that improve people's lives.

One of the companies Dr. Stone created and founded is Joint Juice, a healthy drink that nourishes joints and helps them to continue functioning the way they should. Joint Juice is on the shelves of stores like Walmart, Sam's Club, Costco, and A&P, and over 300 million cans and bottles of Joint Juice have been sold. Joint Juice was recently acquired by Post Holdings.

Dr. Stone also invented Rescue Reel which was cited by Popular Science Magazine as a Best Invention of the Year. Rescue Reel is a rope device that allows people to grapple down burning buildings as tall as 100 stories.

In 1996, Dr. Stone founded a company called CrossCart which became Aperion Biologics, a clinical-stage regenerative medicine firm in San Antonio, Texas. His latest idea, Z-Lig device, allows pig tissue to be used in knee surgeries without rejection. This medical breakthrough is the first non-human biologic method of ACL reconstruction of the knee. Dr. Stone uses pig tissue in the Z-Lig device because pig tissue is plentiful, young, strong, and healthy. Therefore, it is a new and exciting option for Dr. Stone and others in his field.

Another one of Dr. Stone's start-ups is ProPrioSense Holdings, a medical device company combining computers and personal sensors to evaluate patients, permit assessment and enable digital physical therapy remotely, and perform continuous outcome studies without requiring patients to return to Stone's clinic. One of his companies, ReGen Biologics Inc. is now a public company. Dr. Stone's latest start-up is TMatch LLC, a software company whose product, TissueMatch, provides a simplified way for surgeons and hospitals to find donor tissues globally.

Dr. Stone has been able to get very far by constantly being creative and creating one company and product after the other. If you want to start multiple businesses and create multiple products based on what you love, you can!

## Successful Self-Published Authors Are Breaking The Rules

The reason why there are self-published authors getting more sales than authors who use the traditional publishing system is because these self-published authors are able to write more books faster and sell them at ridiculously low prices. Self-published authors can charge $0.99 for their Kindle eBooks to get a big volume of sales, and in some cases, self-published authors are able to charge below $6 for a paperback.

Those are the types of prices that the traditionally published author cannot match. Self-published authors are able to take advantage of the traditional publishing system. However, this advantage is now known to many people. There are many self-published authors who are taking advantage of low prices and being able to publish numerous books every year. Now there are too many self-published authors doing the same thing.

In order to stand out as a self-published author, you need to do something more than charge $0.99 or $2.99 for your books and publish them frequently. Maybe that means putting more content into your books and offering it for the same price, or giving your book as a free gift to the people who buy your training course. The differentiating factor could also be created by simplifying your book with less content and charging the same price.

**The Lamborghini Formula**

When people think of getting a car, the first thing that comes to mind is getting the new car as soon as possible. The car is waiting for you at the dealership, and all you have to do is pay for it. Some cars are $20,000 while other cars are more expensive.

Cars are also made by an assembly line. It seems as if there are less people and more machines making the cars. The machines are a cheaper solution that can make cars 24/7 for 365 days every year. These are the rules that most of the car dealerships go by when they make their cars. Lamborghini is different. Imagine waiting over a year to get your car because the assembly line has no machines. Imagine having to pay well over $100,000 for one Lamborghini. Lamborghini broke the rules of making affordable cars. It is easy to assume that the person cruising in a Lamborghini is very wealthy. Most other cars do not cost nearly as much as Lamborghinis do. By breaking the rules, Lamborghini got to where it is today.

## The Relationship Between
## Creativity And Taking The Leap

There are an infinite amount of ways that you can take the leap. When it comes to taking the leap, you ultimately have two choices. You can either take the leap using traditional methods, or you can take the leap by using methods that no one has tried before. Sometimes, the traditional methods will be the better methods to go with, but at other times, your methods that no one else has tried before are the better way to go. You will never know which of the two is better until you try them both.

In order to identify whether the traditional system or your system is better, implement both of them at two different times for one month. This is similar to a split test. If you are trying to find out which method improves book sales, use the traditional system for one of your books and use your system for the other book. The traditional system is not always wrong, and your system is not always right (and vice versa).

## Brad Hines' Creative Idea That Brought His Own Board Game To Life

As a serial entrepreneur and a business man, creativity has been a driving force for Brad Hines' success. Hines has been involved in product inception, writing, selling, marketing, teaching, designing, consulting, and everything in between. He eventually decided to step out of those niches and create his own board game. Hines invented the board game *Recollection* that was based around a concept he saw in the 90s movie *Phenomenon*. Based on the movie, *Recollection* is a social knowledge board game in which players compete with each other to find out who can recollect things from categories the best. Brad created his board game with TheGameCrafter.com and only spent $50 on the entire project. While other board games are crowdfunded, Brad took another approach that allowed him to spend a small amount of money. *Recollection* is in multiple online stores and continues growing to this day. You can find *Recollection* and other products Brad sells on www.bradfordhines.com/store.

## Bruce Gray's Creative Sculptures
## Attract Large Attention

Bruce Gray is an established Los Angeles metal sculptor and kinetic artist who was interested in creative expression since childhood. During his childhood, Bruce did not take creative expression seriously. In fact, he did not take it seriously until he became an adult. Bruce enlisted himself to the Coast Guard for four years right out of high school. When his term was over, Bruce decided to apply to the University of Massachusetts which was known for its art school. Unfortunately for Bruce, one of the requirements was an art portfolio. He did not have an art portfolio, so he drew one in pencil, and the drawing got denied.

Although that may have looked like the end, the Dean gave Bruce a chance to draw in front of him and possibly have his application reconsidered. Although he was not feeling confident and nearly walked out, Bruce decided to stick with it. The Dean eventually allowed Bruce to attend the University of Massachusetts on a probationary basis meaning Bruce had to keep a B average to stay in. Those four years allowed Bruce to become educated in various forms of art and sculpting.

After Bruce graduated, he got jobs in photography and advertising, but he knew he could do better. He left those jobs behind, and after years of wandering around, getting different jobs, and living in different states, Bruce finally decided to move to Los Angeles in January 1989 and become an artist. At the beginning, Bruce only knew how to sculpt designs with wood, but most of his design ideas needed steel. As a result, Bruce learned how to use steel for his designs and has now become very successful. Bruce's sculptures have appeared in numerous movies, some universities in the United States, the NBC Universal Studios, and other prestigious places. Bruce decided to combine his creativity and love for art into his own sculptures that have amazed thousands. You can see some of Bruce's sculptures at brucegray.com.

## Just Like A Science Experiment

This may sound just like a science experiment, and it should. The hypothesis is whether using Method B will get more sales than Method A. This is similar to A/B Split Testing for a website. Method A is the control, the traditional system that everyone uses. Then, you need to identify the results of implementing Method A (number of sales, conversion rate, etc). At the same time, you need to apply Method B to another product. After a month has gone by, record your results. If Method B got less sales, then there are two possible reasons. Either you chose the wrong method to use or did not effectively promote the product. On the contrary, an increase in sales with Method B would indicate that you need to focus on implementing that method more often.

By finding the conclusion, you will be able to identify whether or not your system is better than the traditional system. People do not commonly think of these actions as a science experiment, but they both shockingly have many things in common. Some people in the front of their stampedes are the scientists who experiment with molecules, plants, liquids, and other things. There are other leaders who are experimenting with products, traffic, social network followers, Klout score, and other things.

By approaching your ideas like experiments, you will be able to find the best solutions faster. However, some methods take more time than others. Some traditional systems remain established for many years until new systems take their place. In order to decide how long your experiment is going to be, you need to decide how long you are willing to wait for a solution. Some solutions will come faster than others.

One of the experiments I came up with immediately showed an increase in blog traffic. The experiment was to go from tweeting every hour to tweeting every half an hour. On the first day I tweeted every half an hour, my blog traffic went up by 25%. My blog traffic continues to exponentially grow to this day, and Twitter is a big reason for that growth.

The hypothesis was whether or not doubling the frequency of my tweets would lead to more visitors on my blog. My conclusion ultimately supported my hypothesis. I will stop sounding like a scientist, but you get the idea.

Experimenting with your products, traffic, sales, and business by thinking of it as a science experiment is a creative way to get better results. Some of those results are going to be very creative. Regardless of whether your hypothesis is right or wrong, you will learn how to improve your business and get the best results possible.

**I Broke A Rule. You're Next**

There are countless examples of people breaking the rules. When a rule is first established, it is thought of as a valuable rule. However, some rules become obsolete with age. The time it takes for a rule to become obsolete varies. It took a long time for people to break the rule of using the traditional publisher while some of the rules about blogging got old fast.

I broke a rule for my niche as well. The rule was that 80% of the content you tweet should be links to other people's blog posts while 20% of the content you tweet should be links to your blog. When I decided to break this rule, I didn't go from 80% of other blogs and 20% of my blog to 70% of other blogs and 30% of my blog. I went from where I was to tweeting about my blog every time with the exception of 4 inspirational quotes throughout the day. Breaking the rule allowed me to see a big increase in traffic for my blog. The visitors coming to my blog doubled overnight. Having a big audience of targeted followers on Twitter did help, but instead of having those targeted followers visit other people's blog posts, they were all visiting my blog and reading the posts there.

My sales did not have an immediate change, but over the long term, I got more book sales because more people were visiting my blog. The people who buy my books commonly talk with me on Twitter. By breaking the rules, my Twitter followers are able to see more of my content, and more people are able to see my products.

That is one of the rules I broke. I have broken many other rules in my niche such as being successful as a teenager. Your niche may be different from mine, or you may be in the same niche as me. Regardless of the niche you are in, there are rules. Some of them are designed to be kept while others are meant to be broken.

By breaking a rule in your niche, people will pay attention to you. Breaking the rules allows you to be creative, and that creativity will allow you to rewrite the rules of your niche. That is a very strong statement, but if you got better results by breaking certain rules and implementing tactics that other experts would never implement, you can rewrite the rules of your niche.

**How Too Many People See The Experts**
Too many people see the experts as people with old tricks that don't work anymore. Some people say things like, "Never trust the experts." Experts are just people who became successful by implementing their own methods. That means some of those methods will work for you while others will not. I felt the need to clear that up because experts get good results by implementing their tactics. You may get better results by implementing different tactics from the experts you know. You may get better results by listening to the experts. Most of the time I break a rule in my niche, I see what the experts implement, and I make some minor changes to what the experts do in order to get a different result. Instead of tweeting every hour, I tweet every

30 minutes. That is a small change that has made a big difference towards my blog's traffic.

Breaking the rules may just be making a small change to a rule that already exists. Making a small change can solve a big problem. We have been taught that the rules are made to stick. Breaking the rules would get us in trouble. This ideology is rightfully enforced at an early age so fewer people participate in illegal activities. However, breaking the long established rules in your niche may allow you to go into unchartered lands and lead the stampede. Break some of the rules that exist in your niche. Then break more of them! Give it a try and see where it takes you.

# Consistency

Consistency is another important characteristic that you need to lead the stampede. Consistency is important because where we are now, failure or success, is not final. Once you become successful and become a leader of your niche, you need to keep your lead by being consistent. If Amazon was not consistent, someone would eventually surpass them. If authors do not consistently write new books, people may forget about them. If bloggers forget to write a blog post for a few months, people may forget about them as well.

Consistency is one of the rules that was not made to be broken. We have valued the importance of consistency throughout our entire lives. We all value consistency in one way or the other to this day. Chances are you have a favorite TV show, and you know the time and date that new shows go live. You may like *The Big Bang Theory*, or you may like another TV show.

At that time and date, you're probably on the couch watching TV and waiting for the new show to start. You are eager to see what happens to your favorite characters, or you're in it for a good laugh, or even both. If the new show is on, you are happy that it's on, and you continue watching. If a repeat is on instead of the new show that you expected, you will most likely be disappointed. Then again, many people watch the repeats anyway.

We always expect a new episode at a certain time and a certain day of the week. We expect this consistency to always be met. When your favorite show goes from airing at 9 pm to airing at 5 am, chances are you won't be happy about it. You won't want to wake up that early just to watch your favorite TV show. Changing the time of a TV show to that extent will ruin the consistency of that show's airing on a certain time and day. Some people would even get disappointed if their favorite TV show went from being aired at 9 pm to being aired at 10 pm on the same day.

We will never escape our need for consistency since we are creatures of habit. If you hire employees, you expect them to consistently perform well. If you are a business owner, you want results that are consistently on the rise. Now that we have established why consistency is important and how it affects our daily lives, it is time to implement that consistency into your business.

## Consistency In Action: The Debate About Blogging Frequency

Being consistent is beneficial in many areas, and one of those areas is blogging. Blogging is a fun way to allow people to read your content for free. As blogging becomes more popular, more of the tips for successful blogging have been filled with controversy. One of the controversial tips is blogging frequency. Some bloggers recommend publishing one post every day while others say that blogging once a week is the way to go. I send out multiple blog posts every week, and there are plenty of other frequencies to choose from. I would recommend blogging at least once a day, but there are many perspectives towards this one tip.

The best way to look at blogging frequency is to blog at a consistent rate that brings forth valuable content. Whether that means sending out a blog post every day or every week, be consistent. If you only send blog posts out on a Thursday, send them all out on Thursdays. If you send out your blog posts every day at 10 am, then you always need to publish a blog post at 10 am every day.

By being consistent, people will know when to expect your blog posts. Some people expect to get notified about a new blog post at 6:30 am while others expect to be notified about a blog post a few hours later. Some people publish their blog posts late into the night. Regardless of when you are publishing your blog posts, it is important to publish your blog post when people are expecting them.

**Consistency In Action: Restaurants**
Another great example of consistency in action is in restaurants. At any restaurant, you can expect a waiter or waitress to come up to you with a menu. If you have visited the same restaurant multiple times, you also expect your favorite entree to be on the menu every time.

When we visit the same restaurant multiple times, we also expect the quality of the food to be consistent. If you have visited a restaurant 10 times, and you enjoyed the food all 10 times, you would also expect to enjoy the food on the 11th time you go to that restaurant. Chefs of the most successful restaurants live up to that expectation every time and deliver on a consistent basis.

Fast food restaurants are consistent at providing food quicker than the traditional restaurant. Every time you go to a fast food restaurant in your area, you expect to have a hamburger within 5-10 minutes. In order to get returning customers, restaurants consistently send out the food at the right time and provide us with the value we want.

## Consistency Creates Expectations

The reason consistency is a powerful element towards leading the stampede is because clients begin to expect something at a certain time. Just like we expect the new episode to air at a certain time, clients begin to expect products, content, and services within a certain amount of time. If you are consistent for a month, many of your clients will expect that consistency to last. On the one day the new episode is not at its scheduled time, people expecting the new episode will not be pleased about the unpleasant surprise. Just as it would be an unpleasant surprise for a new episode to be delayed, it would also be an unpleasant surprise for an Amazon Prime member to get his order five days later. Amazon Prime members pay for free two day shipping. If that consistency is broken, Amazon Prime members won't be happy.

Being consistent long enough creates the expectation that the consistency will be endless. When people expect you to publish a blog post or create a new product, you need to fulfill those expectations. If people expect a daily blog post, then you need to write one blog post every day. You can go above and beyond the call of duty by publishing two blog posts every day. However, by consistently writing two blog posts every day for a long period of time will result in two daily blog posts becoming the expectation. You have upped your standards, and now the people who know about you expect those standards to be kept. Once you establish yourself for doing something consistently, the only two good options you have is to consistently provide what you are providing or going the extra mile. You want to go the extra mile because customers remember the people who over deliver. They remember the people who gave them the extra time, the extra product, or the extra service. Customers do not remember the average person because there are so many average people. That is why you need to stand out, and going the extra mile is one of the best ways to stand out in your niche.

**Why Expectations Are Important**
We have expectations for certain things that happen in our lives. We expect certain results, certain events to occur, and certain weather. If the meteorologist says there will be sunny skies on Tuesday, then that is exactly what we expect on Tuesday. There are other days when the meteorologists tell us about the impending snow storm. As a result, everyone is rushing over to the grocery stores to get their last minute shopping done before the big storm hits. We expect our expectations to be met, and that is why they are so important.
We do not respond well to change. If it rains when it was supposed to be sunny, that creates a problem for many

people. Runners who wanted to run outside will have to adjust their schedules so they can run after the rain stops or just run on the treadmill. The people at the local beach get an unpleasant surprise when the rainstorm strikes the area. There are a lot of things that can go wrong when meteorologists make the wrong predictions.

We are creatures of habit. There are some things that we do every day, and some of those things are considered as second nature. We have our own daily rituals, and if those daily rituals get interrupted, we do not respond well to those interruptions. Some of the things we do every day are brush our teeth (please tell me you do this), eat food, sleep, and other activities depending on the individual.

The reason we do not like change is because change is a scary process to go through. Change brings forth uncertainty, and in many cases, uncertainty also results in fear. Since we do not like change, we also do not like it when our expectations are not met. There are some days when I run a race, expect a certain time, and then finish 10 seconds slower than that time. It's not a good feeling.

Your business needs to fulfill the expectations that you have been able to fulfill in the past. If your business is known for effective social media services, you need to constantly fulfill that expectation. If your business is not known for fashion consulting, you do not need to fulfill that expectation.

**Choosing The Right Expectations To Fulfill**
Not all expectations are equal. Some expectations are
going to be easy for you to fulfill while others are going to
be a bit more challenging. In order to fulfill your clients'
expectations, you need to choose the right expectations to
offer and implement. These are the three factors that will
help you decide which expectations are the right ones to
fulfill for your clients.

1. **How much time it takes to fulfill the expectation.** If it
   takes weeks to fulfill one client's expectations, you will
   encounter a problem with time when you have hundreds
   of clients who have the same expectations. Choose the
   expectations that do not take too long to fulfill. If you still
   need to fulfill these kinds of expectations, price these
   services at a point where few clients would buy them.
   These kinds of expectations, the ones that take weeks to
   fulfill, are the ones that you only want to provide to a few
   people, not a few hundred people.
2. **How good you are at fulfilling the expectation.** The
   client chose you. There are plenty of other competitors
   offering the same services. How good you are at fulfilling
   certain expectations for your clients will determine how
   many of those clients buy something else from you in the
   future. If you are not good at fulfilling a certain
   expectation, do not tell your clients that you can fulfill that
   expectation. It is okay to tell a client you cannot do
   something.
3. **The benefit of fulfilling the expectation.** What does
   fulfilling the expectation bring you? Does it result in more

traffic, more sales, achieving your ultimate purpose in life, or something else? You want to benefit from putting in the hard work to fulfill your clients' expectations. Organize the expectations you fulfill so you are able to identify which ones have the biggest impact on you and your clients.

**Less Is More**
These three factors will help you choose the expectations that are worth fulfilling. Some people will have a list of 10 expectations to fulfill while other people may have a smaller list. Too many people feel as if they will get more sales if they fulfill more expectations.
By fulfilling more expectations, time gets scattered. Expectations are fulfilled, but those fulfillments are subpar. A smaller list brings forth more value. Only offering your clients three options will allow you to focus in on those three options and get really good at fulfilling your clients' expectations. Giving your clients less choices will result in happier clients because you are able to go beyond their expectations and fulfill specific needs and wants.

**Going Beyond Expectation**
Consistency is important to keep, but you will find some opportunities to break the consistency in a good way. When you decide to go beyond expectation, your clients will be very grateful. People expect the consistency to last. You can surprise your clients with a random giveaway or consult with them for an extra hour free of charge.

The only reason you should break consistency is to go beyond your clients' expectations. After you go beyond their expectations, continue to provide the same expectations at a consistent rate. Going beyond expectations allows you to test out different things. If a giveaway does not work the way you wanted it to, you do not have to consistently host giveaways. You can host them sporadically and keep on testing them until you know that your giveaways will be successful. Then, you can decide whether or not you will host giveaways at a consistent rate.

Going beyond expectations is the only way you should break consistency. I broke my consistency of publishing one blog post every day by publishing two blog posts on a single day. I tested this out for a month, liked the results I saw, and now I publish two blog posts every day. I broke the consistency of tweeting every hour, decided to tweet every 30 minutes, and liked the results I saw. Even then, I found ways to tweet more often, and now I send out a tweet once every 20 minutes.

## Broken Consistency Gets Noticed

Amazon is known for being super-fast at delivering its products, especially for Amazon Prime members. I will never forget ordering something on Amazon that took over a month to arrive at my house. This was not Amazon's fault because I ordered from a third party seller, but waiting a month for something that normally arrived in a week was not an experience I would like to forgo again. Broken consistency does get noticed. Clients complain about the broken consistency. Clients who are dissatisfied are more likely to say something than the clients who are happy with your product. Businesses that have broken their consistency tend to get more complaints from their clients. Then, those complaints find their way on the internet. An example of complaints finding their way on the internet would be the Comcast customer service employee who went viral for giving one of his clients a really hard time. Once you are established for being consistent at something, you need to stay consistent in that area. If you break the consistency, you break other people's expectations. This is why it is important to go beyond expectations when you choose to break consistency.

### The Leaders Of Your Niche Are Doing Some Things Consistently

The leader of your niche is doing something consistently. The leaders of the blogging niche are consistently publishing 1 blog post every day. The leaders of social media are the ones with targeted followings, and the big blue check mark showing that your account is verified does help. The leaders of your niche are consistently fulfilling their clients' expectations.

In order to become a leader of your niche, you need to perform some things consistently. Sending out a tweet, publishing a blog post, and creating a new product are some of the things that you can do consistently. Ask yourself what you can do consistently to improve your business and write them in your notebook.

## Consistency+Frequency=The Perfect Blueprint

Being consistent can mean a wide variety of things. Consistency means publishing 1 blog post every day, but it can also mean publishing 1 blog post every month. Both are examples of being consistent, but publishing 1 blog post every day leads to more traffic than publishing 1 blog post every month. This is when frequency comes in. Being consistent is the starting point of achievement, but increasing your frequency will allow more people to recognize your consistency. The bloggers who publish 1 blog post every day get noticed for consistency and frequency.

Combining both consistency and frequency together leads to what I like to call the perfect storm. The perfect blueprint is when you are getting visitors, subscribers, and sales from all of the corners of the internet because they know when you will come out with a new update and that the update will come soon. I am consistently publishing multiple books every year. The people who enjoy my books know that more books are on the way. The people who enjoy Apple's iPhone know that a new one comes out every year. Some people have five old iPhones in their collection because Apple is consistently producing new iPhones that more people want every time.

The perfect blueprint makes clients less likely to leave. If someone creates a training course every month, and you don't like January's training course, you may like the training course offered in February. If people don't like the blog post they got today, they won't unsubscribe because a new blog post is going to get published the next day.

Once the perfect blueprint is in action, the last factor that comes in play is value. The value of a product will determine how many people become returning customers and tell other people about you. When your customers tell other people about you via word of mouth, they will be spreading your message, products, and services to more people. Word of mouth marketing is a big component that results in a big increase in your traffic, subscribers, and sales.

These upward statistics indicate that what you are doing is working and that your Perfect Blueprint is working. Thinking about the Perfect Blueprint is the easy part, but getting it to happen is the hard part. Making the Perfect Blueprint happen requires time, patience, and work. Some people give up right when they are about to get great results from their Perfect Blueprints because great results can come at any given moment. No one gets to look into the crystal ball and know when those results are coming. It is up to you to stick with the journey and learn new techniques so you can make those results happen sooner. By combining good consistency with good frequency, you will have the Perfect Blueprint that will allow you to get the results that you have always dreamed of.

# The Ability To Know What Is Important

It seems as if the world keeps on giving us tasks to do. However, not every task has the same importance. Some tasks are more important than others. For example, scheduling tweets is important, but it is more important to be on the webinar you told everyone you would be a special guest on. Finding people to connect with is important, but it is more important to write a blog post that you know needs to be published within 30 minutes.

You are going to encounter many options and opportunities, but they are not created equal. People who lead their stampedes know what is important and make the right choices. If an opportunity won't lead to big results, the leaders say no. In fact, leaders say no more than they say yes. Leaders only say yes to the opportunities that yield the highest return from the time invested into that opportunity.

## The Dip Factor

Seth Godin has written numerous *New York Times* bestselling books, and one of them is *The Dip*. *The Dip* tells people when they should quit and when they should stick. When you combine consistency and frequency together, that is also going to equal a big investment in your time. You may also have to invest money and other resources to be consistent and frequent at the same time.

The main takeaway from *The Dip* is to not bother investing your time into something when you know it is not going to work. You don't want to invest a lot of time into something and then realize all of your hard work was in vain. It is better to spend your time sticking with something and getting the results versus sticking with something, realizing that the results are not coming in, and then give up on it after investing your time and resources. You don't want to come to the conclusion that it is not going to work years after you started. You want to find out whether or not something is going to work as soon as you encounter it. There are only so many things that we can consistently and frequently do. In order to get the best out of your time, you need to be picky about your options. Some options will be better than others. You should weigh the pros and cons of one of your ideas before you start so you know whether it will be worthwhile or not. You should focus on implementing ideas that you feel confidence about. It is better to continue investing your time in the things that you know how to do very well than it is to try something that you are not confident about.

**Experimenting With New Things**
Innovation is an important aspect of leading the stampede, and being innovative does involve approaching new things. If you believe in your ability to be successful at something, give it a try. However, if you quickly realize you made the wrong decision, it is entirely okay to back down from that decision. It is also important to not back down just because the adversity and obstacles are too challenging. No matter what you pursue, you will encounter adversity and

obstacles. If you enjoy what you are doing and are good at it, stick with it through the obstacles and the triumphs. When you try something new for the first time, you should not invest as much time into that new thing as you already invest in your priorities. Out of all of my social networks, I invest most of my time on Twitter, and the results prove it. I have far more Twitter followers than I have followers on any other social network. I decided to give Pinterest a try. Initially, I did not invest a lot of time in Pinterest because Twitter was already bringing me good results. As I started to see Pinterest bringing in results, and I became good at using that social network, then I decided to invest a good portion of my time into Pinterest. Now I also invest some of my time into Instagram and Facebook, but no matter what happens, I will invest most of my time into Twitter.

We will have to experiment with new things, but before you go into something new, think of the dip factor. With almost everything, there is a grind we must go through. While we are going through that grind, some days will yield good results while other days will yield bad ones. Then, by being consistent and frequent, the perfect storm will come, and you will see a big, positive change in your results.

The Dip Factor is not designed to prevent you from trying new things. Instead, it is designed to make you think about the consequences--good or bad--about your decision before you make that decision. You don't want to approach something new, invest too much time into it, and end up giving up on it after you have invested so much time into that decision.

## Why We Like New Things

When something is new, we tend to like it a lot. The new sneakers look twice as good as the ones that were thrown in the back of the closet 6 months ago. There are many cases in which something new is a good change. It is an enhancement from the old version.

There are always going to be sneakers that come out that look better than ever. When people get new sneakers, some of these people think they have the best sneakers around. When the sneakers get old, they get replaced by another new pair. Then, that new pair that replaced the old sneakers (that was new at one point) is now the big deal. The new things look like the best options. However, as the new become old, their status of being best slips away. Soon, there is an even better option.

The iPhone is a powerful device that millions of people have. Remember when the iPhone 4S was the big thing? The iPhone 4S was the newest iPhone because it came with Siri, loaded super fast, and it was the last iPhone Steve Jobs' created. Let's flash forward to the year after that. The iPhone 5 dominates the market because it's got an inch or so on the 4S. At this time, the iPhone 5 is the next big thing. In 2013, The iPhone 5C and iPhone 5S came out with the finger print authorization. There's no longer a need for a 4 digit password. Your finger print is unique, and no one can take that away from you. It's also really cool as both a gadget and a way to show off to your friends. There were a variety of colors to choose from, especially with the iPhone 5C. As a result, the iPhone 5 got pushed to the back of the line.

The new is only new until something surpasses it, or you have had it for a while. When I started to write this book, the iPhone 5C and iPhone 5S were the must-have iPhones. Alas, the iPhone 6C and 6S are now the next must-have iPhones, and some people are already talking about the next rumored iPhones. As a result, the iPhone 5C and iPhone 5S have been pushed to the back of the line.

Being up to date allows us to show off to all of the other people who are not as up to date. This sounds like a trait that a select few have--the ability to be boastful--but we all like to show other people our up to date technology and products. A friend showed me his iPhone 5S in action. He put his finger on the square, and the iPhone automatically opened. There was no 4 digit code or a slide and swipe. It was just my friend's finger that unlocked his iPhone 5S. The funny thing is that I (and everyone else nearby) watched him do the same thing three times. We did not object to him locking and unlocking his iPhone 5S three times. We wanted to see the new iPhone in action just as much as anyone else who already has an iPhone.

Another reason why we like new things is that we cannot escape them. There are millions of people with the new iPhone 5C and iPhone 5S. One of those people could be (and is most likely) one of your friends. All they have to do is take out their iPhone, tell you it's an iPhone 5S, and either you or one of your friends will immediately ask a question about the iPhone 5S. What does finger print verification look like? Is the iPhone 5S faster than the 4S? Is the iPhone 5S shorter or longer than the iPhone 5? Does the camera for the iPhone 5S look better than the iPhone 5? Those are some of the many questions that can come up in a typical conversation. Whether your friend tells you this directly or indirectly, that friend is most likely going to tell you that the iPhone 5S is much better than any of the other iPhones before it. You probably knew that already, but your friend gets the ability to reinforce that, and you let that friend do so.

The person with the iPhone 5S becomes popular. Everyone is asking him questions about it and asking him to do the finger print verification 'one final time.' The longer you stay with that friend and talk about the iPhone 5S, the more likely you are to end up buying the 5S or another iPhone in the future. That's because the iPhone 5S sounds like something beyond your wildest dreams. The iPhone 5S seems at least 10 times better than your iPhone because of these three reasons:

1. **You don't have the iPhone 5S** (and if you do, you probably showed it off to a few people). We tend to want the new things that we don't have because they are usually better than what we already have. In addition, everyone wants to brag about themselves as much as possible.
2. **Your friend or acquaintance showed it off**. Even if your friend decides to not allow anyone to look at or touch his iPhone 5S, you will end up becoming curious and plead with your friend to see the iPhone 5S. Even if

you do not plead, your friend almost feels obligated to show off his new iPhone 5S. Therefore, the loophole cannot be avoided.

3. **Your iPhone suddenly looks as old as The Stone Age**. Four years is the difference between no Siri and an iPhone with Siri and finger print verification to unlock the screen. While your friend tells you about how awesome the iPhone 5S is, you can't help but look down at your outdated iPhone and start to realize how outdated it is.

That's the truth about it. We can't resist the new because it tends to be an upgrade from what we have. The new is usually better than the old. Some old things are better than new things, but new products stand out. That's how Apple sells millions of its new iPhones minutes after they go up for sale. Outgrowing the need for something new--whether it be a new food, phone, car, or book--is something that is almost impossible to outgrow. It is rooted deep into our minds in childhood, and its roots keep on digging in as we get older and see more new things. The first computer was the next big thing a long time ago, in a galaxy far, far away. Now we have laptops that are much faster than the old computers and have a lot more functions as well. Those old computers used to be new. Many computers later, those computers that were once new have become ancient. We like new things, and that's exactly why you need to always have a new product or service available.

## Materialistic New Vs New Goals

We like new things that look better than the old. The materialistic need for newness comes in the form of the newest smartphone, the newest computer, the newest car, the newest sneakers, and any other new things that you get or want. New goals are a completely different kind of new. Some new goals look just as shiny as the iPhone 5S while other goals look as dull as the very first computer (nothing against the first computer for a collector, but the first computer in today's world would be very slow).

Although certain new goals will look incredible at first, some of them may lose their shine as you go through the dip process. You will realize the amount of work you have to put in. You will realize how much time (and in numerous cases, money) you will have to invest in order to accomplish your goal. Before encountering the dip, you need to look beyond the shine of the goal. Depending on the goal, accomplishing that goal may take a few hours, a few days, a few weeks, a few months, or a few years. Many people give up on their goals because a month later, as work increases, the goal looks more difficult to attain. Writing a blog post every day seems easy for the first few days of most new bloggers. However, as that work consistently gets performed over a long period of time, some bloggers back out. In addition, getting low traffic in the beginning despite all of the hard work is yet another common reason why new bloggers back out. By backing out from blogging, those people wasted hours or even days trying to maintain a blog that they decided to give up on.

Before choosing a goal, make sure the shine of the goal is always there, and make sure this is a goal that you can attain. Backing out during the dip will turn all of your invested time into nothing. It is better not to start something at all than it is to invest a lot of time in something and then back out.

## Opportunities!

We love getting them. When we get an opportunity, that means someone has faith in us. When someone asks you to write a guest post, that's an opportunity. That person has faith in you! We seem to want to grasp as many opportunities as we can get. More opportunities equates to more visibility. However, not all opportunities are created equal. Some opportunities will be better than others. One guest blogging site may have 10,000 daily readers while the other guest blogging site may have 25,000 readers. One public event may have 100 registrants while another public event may have 1,000 registrants. If you are a public speaker, which public event would you prefer to be speaking at?

When it comes to an opportunity, the number of people is not the primary way to decide whether one option is better than the other. Let's say that you are organizing the public event. Speaker A has 100,000 followers on Twitter while Speaker B has 10,000 followers on Twitter. If you could only choose one of them, which one would you prefer? The number of followers someone has is not enough to make a good decision. In order to choose the best opportunities possible, you need to do some research.

Let's say Speaker A bought 100,000 followers for $75, and that's why that speaker looks so popular. This artificial growth makes Speaker A *look* more influential than Speaker B, and a tool like TwitterAudit could nail people like Speaker A. Maybe Speaker B does a better job at interacting with his followers than Speaker A. It is also possible that Speaker A does not have a targeted following while all of Speaker B's followers are targeted. It is also possible that Speaker B has a higher Klout score than Speaker A.

Those are some of the things you could research in order to decide which of the two speakers would be better for your event. People like to make themselves look bigger than they really are. The blogger who gets 100 daily visitors may say that the blog rakes up 500 daily visitors just to get more opportunities. Some people have resorted to lying in order to appear to be just as good as their competition. There is no way to fake leading the stampede. You either lead the stampede or you are doing what you can to claim the leader spot.

In the beginning, opportunities will not come as often, and grasping any opportunity is a good feat. As you get more opportunities, you need to choose the ones that you are going to invest the most time into. Some opportunities will allow you to make more connections. As you make more connections, you will also get more opportunities. It is easy to imagine how much time this will take.

When choosing your opportunities, you also need to consider the importance of your work. Writing a 1,000 word guest post a day would be very hectic for me since I already write 2 blog posts a day, write books, schedule tweets, and do many other things as well. When the opportunities become overwhelming and produce a result that is not worth the schedule changes you need to make, that opportunity is no longer worth the effort.

When an opportunity gets in the way of the work you do, it reduces your business' growth. I used to write a guest post every other day. I traded those guest posts for better and longer books. I traded surfing the internet for connecting with my followers on Twitter. I traded a large portion of time I spent playing video games to record YouTube videos. Trading that time also gave me some extra time to read books.

**Your Annual Peak Point Of Opportunity**
We all have a certain time of year that we get and can respond to the most opportunities. For me, that would be the summer. No school means 7 extra hours to write books, respond to people's emails, write blog posts, build connections, and teach my Teenager Entrepreneur bootcamp to numerous teens in New York. By knowing your annual peak point, whether December is your big month or spring is your big season, you will know what time you will be able to respond to the most opportunities.

By knowing your annual peak point, you will be able to identify at what time of the year your business will experience the biggest growth. By knowing the time of year your business will get a big increase in sales, you will be able to identify that month or season as the most important one of them all. This does not mean all of the other months and seasons are not important. The annual peak point of opportunity is like the 4th quarter of the Super Bowl. The first three quarters were important, but the 4th quarter is the most important of them all.

## Simplification Makes Everything Easier

There will be a point when giving up looks like the only option. Sometimes, giving up allows you to focus on the things that are more important towards your business' growth. The problem with many entrepreneurs is that they give themselves too many goals that they need to accomplish in order to achieve their vision. They give themselves 10 goals in order to achieve the one vision of getting more blog traffic.

A simpler method will allow entrepreneurs to still get the results they are looking for, but in less time. Being on every social network is not an effective strategy, but building a powerful presence on one or two social networks is an effective strategy. Investing more time into different social networks makes the process of getting to the vision more complex. Focusing on one or two social networks allows the vision of the goal to be crystal clear.

If you can get the same job done with 5 goals, there is no reason to give yourself 5 more goals to get the same result. You don't even need a 6th goal if all you need are five goals to get the job done. By having less goals, you will be able to focus in on those goals and get them done more effectively. It is better to have 1,000 followers on one social network than it is to have 50 followers on 20 social networks. By simplifying everything, you can interact with 1,000 people on one platform versus having to interact with 1,000 people on 20 different platforms.

Simplification will allow you to identify what is truly important. This concept will change the mindset from having a large quantity of goals to having high quality goals. More goals do not mean better results. More goals simply make the process of achieving the vision take longer. Some visions will require 10 goals to achieve, but if you can achieve the same vision with 5 goals, or even with 9 goals, make the change. Simplifying your plan will make the entire process easier for you, and making the process easier will give you more confidence to stick with the goal.

Another simple way to make everything easier is to designate the first three hours of your day to work on your business. If you have to work on any products, grow your social media presence, or anything else for the good of your business, spend the first three hours of your day doing that. Unless you are customer support (not to be confused with an entrepreneur who just does everything for his business), do not look at your inbox at all. You will be amazed with how this simple approach can help you be more productive.

# Persistence

In order to lead the stampede, you need to have persistence. Once you choose something that you know you can accomplish, you need to stick with it. Many people give up on their dreams too early. You never know how close you are towards accomplishing your dreams until you accomplish them. You may be one connection away from turning your dream into a reality. A door may open for you that you didn't even know was there. In order to get opportunities you did not expect and to accomplish your goals, you need to be persistent.

Persistence is one of the more obvious traits among all leaders. You don't simply show up at the front of the stampede. While implementing the other characteristics will allow you to lead the stampede, you get there with persistence. It takes persistence to get up and continue after being rejected. It takes persistence to get up after getting really bad statistics and keep on going. It takes persistence to make everything you want to happen come true.

This is why you need to think about the dip factor before choosing your goals. You need to choose the goals that you know you will be able to accomplish. Being persistent for the wrong goals and for the wrong reasons will not allow you to lead the stampede. When choosing a goal, be sure to choose a goal that you can easily be persistent with and have fun with at the same time.

**3 Helpful Ways To Stay Persistent**

If being persistent was easy, everyone would be persistent. Unfortunately, being persistent is downright difficult. There will be thoughts in your mind that say, "I can't do this, I'm not qualified, and if only I were that person instead, then I would be qualified." For some people, persistence comes as second nature, but for others, being persistent is very difficult. In order to have persistence come as a second nature to you, work on these three things:

1. **Your mindset**. Your mindset is critical towards your success. There are many inspirational quotes from famous people such as, "You become what you believe" from Oprah and "Whether you think you can or you can't, you're right" from Henry Ford. Earl Nightingale and others have said the same thing in a different way. Your mindset is one of the factors that decides how persistent you are when you approach the obstacles.

2. **A better response to denial and criticism**. No matter what niche you pursue or how successful you become, there will be a critic. Every athlete has their fair share of critics. Startups have their fair share of critics. Well established entrepreneurs (including the billionaires) have their fair share of critics. There are only two ways to respond to criticism. You either let the critic's words get to your head and ruin your work, or you can ignore the critics and focus on creating products that are based upon what your supporters say about you. Authors who focus on pleasing the people who gave them 1 star reviews will displease the people who gave 5 star

reviews for the same book. Knowing what is important is another characteristic of leaders, and in order to respond to criticism properly, you need to know which of the two audiences is more important: the critics or your supporters. Just to make sure everything is crystal clear, the supporters are more important than the critics.

3. **Dream big or go home**. People like to tell themselves that there is an in-between. The in-between thought is just a substitute for giving up and settling. If you want to be persistent, you have to dream big and know that you are destined for greatness. All you need to do is unlock your potential by being persistent and keep at it.

## Acquiring The Right Mindset

The right mindset is critical towards persistence, time management, and implementing all of the other characteristics as well. For some people, acquiring the right mindset will require a thinking shift. The attitude some people have is the victim attitude. These people believe that they were never destined to be successful or amount to anything in their life. These people simply give up because they believe they are unworthy. As a result, productivity dips downward and less work gets done. The work that does get done is subpar at best.

You need to flip that mindset around from the victim's mindset to the victor's mindset. One of the people who I listen to for many hours is Joel Osteen who constantly emphasizes having the right mindset one way or the other. Joel Osteen is a preacher who uses stories and examples to convey a message. One of those messages was to have the right mindset in which he said to, "Reprogram your computer."

Joel went on to say about how fast and reliable a new computer is. However, the viruses make a computer slow and unreliable. By getting rid of the viruses, the computer becomes fast and reliable again. Then, he compared the computer to our mindset. The viruses are all of the discouraging thoughts we think about that prevent us from being persistent. The viruses result in a negative attitude shift that impacts the way we work and live our lives. By reprogramming your computer (mindset) and getting rid of the viruses (discouraging thoughts), you will be able to be more persistent.

Getting rid of the discouraging thoughts, or at least not focusing on those thoughts, does take some time. The first thing you need to do is be kind and helpful to the people around you. The best way to help yourself and make yourself feel better is by helping someone else. By helping others, you will encounter the sweet spot within your mind that makes you feel significant. When others thank you for what you have done, you feel significant and important.

By feeling significant and important, you will be able to stay persistent. Now that you know you are significant and important, your work takes on a greater meaning. Instead of believing you are just another person in the stampede, you believe that you are someone who people see as significant and important.

In order to have the right mindset, you cannot merely live to seek approval from others. Many people need to be accepted by others in order to continue creating quality products and providing services. Once these people encounter denial, productivity slows down. Then, it takes a few days or even weeks before these people can be productive at the same level before they faced denial. There is a voluminous amount of denial, rejection, and criticism at the front of the stampede. People at the front of the stampede get scrutinized more often and in more detail than anyone else. This close level of inspection and an increase in critics makes many people afraid from leading their stampedes. That creates the fear of getting noticed, and this type of fear is a big problem. We see people criticizing everything imaginable such as the way celebrities dress, how they eat, and who they hang out with. We also see millionaires getting criticized for new business ventures that are not working out as well. Some of those millionaires end up becoming billionaires, but alas, the critics do not go away. Many people do not want to be trapped in constant criticism. Some are afraid to get denied or face rejection. However, if you are being criticized and getting rejected, it means you are doing something right. People are not criticizing the Joe Schmo's of the world. One of the constants in history that happened, is happening, and will happen in the future is that the President will get criticized. They are getting criticized because they are not the Joe Schmo's of the world. They are getting criticized because they are important.

There have been many people who faced rejection and denial, but their persistence allowed them to overcome all of the rejection and denial they received. These are some examples of people who were able to rise above rejection and ended up becoming very successful in their niches.

**The 13th Time Is The Charm**
J.K. Rowling is now a billionaire, but she used to be poor. Then, a giant series of books and movies all about someone named Harry Potter allowed her to go from rags to riches. There are now millions of Harry Potter fans, and there are also plenty of people who have read all of the books and seen all of the movies.
Her first manuscript got denied 12 times. Rowling could have given up after the first denial. That's what many people do because that's the easier thing to do. Getting denied a second time only made things worse for Rowling. After getting denied 7 times, J.K. Rowling could have easily thought Harry Potter was a bust. She could have given up after getting denied by the 12th publisher. However, if she gave up on the 12th publisher, she wouldn't have gotten to Publisher #13 who gave her a chance. That chance turned her into a billionaire.

*To Think I Saw It on Mulberry Street*
Theodore Giesel was denied by 27 different publishers for his book. That is more than twice the number of publishers who rejected Rowling. Giesel could have given up, but the 28th publisher decided to give his book a chance. You may

not remember anyone named Theodore Giesel who was a successful author. That's because Theodore Giesel decided to use the pen name Dr. Seuss for his books.

## The Book That Sold Like Crazy
This particular book got denied by 28 different publishers. After getting denied many times, John Grisham's book, *A Time To Kill* was finally accepted. It is easy to imagine the discouraging thoughts entering Grisham's mind saying that the book would never be accepted. *A Time To Kill* ended up selling over 250 million copies. I'm sure the other 28 publishers who denied him regret their decisions.

## Cut From The High School Basketball Team
When you think of the best basketball player, you would usually think that the athlete played since elementary school, made it on the high school team, played in college, and made it to the NBA. One person who got cut from a high school team was none other than Michael Jordan who is the best basketball player to have ever played the game.

## The 303rd Time Is The Charm
That's how many times it took for Walt Disney to get the financing to create Disney World. It is crazy to even imagine one person could have enough persistence to get one yes after 302 people said no to him. Getting Disney World allowed Walt Disney to establish himself as a leader of his niche.

## 302 Is Plenty, But What About 10,000?

If you thought getting denied 302 times was bad enough, Thomas Edison had it worse. Although Edison was not denied by 10,000 different people, it took Edison over 10,000 tries to make one of his inventions finally work. That invention ended up becoming the light bulb which we encounter every day of our lives in some way or another.

## When Denial Enters Our Lives

There are countless examples of people who faced many denials but became successful in the end. There is going to be a time when denial enters your life. Someone will not like your product. Someone will say that your idea is never going to succeed. There will even be people who say that *you* won't succeed.

Throughout their respective processes, Thomas Edison, Walt Disney, and many others encountered people who said those things to them. One reporter asked Edison how it felt to fail 1,000 times. Edison responded by saying he did not fail 1,000 times. Instead, he referred to the light bulb as an invention with 1,000 steps. Edison's attitude towards his challenge is the right attitude to have when we are facing our own challenges.

You can read more examples about people becoming successful after numerous denials, but there will be a point when you will have to walk the walk. People will deny you. People will say bad things about your products and services. No matter how good you make your products, there will always be a complaint. It is the response towards those complaints that will allow you to be successful and thrive despite the difficulty.

**Focus On The Supporters You Already Have**
When denial enters your life, know that there are people out there who agree with and like what you are doing. Whether your supporters only consist of family and friends, or you have thousands of people who support you, there are people who could not imagine rejecting your products and services.

It is better to ignore the critics than it is to overthink the entire situation. Some people remain stagnate for days after someone says that the product is never going to sell or that the idea will flop. In many cases, the reason critics criticize other people's products is because the critics cannot see the master plan. Many entrepreneurs were criticized for their products, but after implementing an incredible strategy and focusing on the supporters, some of the critics go away.

Too many people make the mistake of shaping their businesses and lives based on what the critics have said. Instead of shaping your business and life based upon what critics say to you, shape your business and life based on the way you want to shape it combined with what your supporters have to say. By creating a lifestyle or business based on what the critics have to say, you will scare away a lot of your supporters and live an unfulfilling life. You should not please the critic at the cost of losing vision, your most loyal customers, and your own happiness.

## Critics Never Go Away

No matter what you do and no matter how successful you become, the critics will not go away. Many entrepreneurs are trying to escape criticism by playing it safe and becoming irrelevant. These entrepreneurs end up staying on the ground never to move up. Instead of trying to escape criticism, you are better off embracing it. There are countless ways criticism will make its way into your life and other people's lives as well. The saying goes, "Don't judge a book by its cover," but people are constantly judging books by their covers. People are judging anything they find that can be judged. In addition, it is easier for people to let others know about their judgments. The food at the local restaurant gets judged, and the review gets posted on Yelp. Products get reviewed on Amazon. Local newspapers and well-known magazines review products.

Critics are inevitable for any business that wants to become successful. It is a fact that we need to understand when we create products and services. There is no sense in trying to escape criticism because the critics always find you. That's because they have nothing else better to do. Each time a critic leaves, another critic takes that person's place.

The reason no one can escape the critics is because no one is perfect. You can't be everything for everyone. It is a proven fact. Some people love their Android smartphone, but the people who use iPhones long enough disdain every other Smartphone in the market. Embrace the world of criticism and rejection because it is there and it's coming for you either way. So you might as well take a firm step forward and persevere through the criticism.

**Overcoming The 1 Star Review**
An overwhelming majority of products have at least one reviewer that only gave the product 1 star. If not, that product was either extremely good or does not get enough attention. When people think of 1 star reviews they think of dissatisfied customers. If there is an accumulation of 1 star reviews but no 4 or 5 star reviews, then the product needs to be revamped. However, if the product has numerous 4 and 5 star reviews and gets a 1 star review, that does not mean the product is bad. That just means your product probably fell into the hands of a customer who did not know how to utilize it properly or is not a part of your target audience. As you continue creating products for your target audience and allow the 1 star reviewers to realize they are not your targeted audience, you will be able to get more 4 and 5 star reviews for your products.

The 1 star review is not the end of a product. It is okay to get a 1 star review. In fact, many products get them. As long as you have many 4 and 5 star reviews from the people who enjoy your products, you have a targeted audience that matters. Do not focus on the 1 star reviewers. Those reviewers are just like the critics. Create products that the 4 and 5 star reviewers will enjoy because that is your target audience. There is no point in trying to partially satisfy a 1 star reviewer's complaint at the cost of losing the people who gave good reviews.

**Believe In Your Ability To Be Successful**
In order to be successful, you first need to believe that you can get there. Believing that you will be successful is critical towards staying persistent. Walt Disney believed Disney World would be successful. Thomas Edison believed in the light bulb. Michael Jordan believed in his ability to play basketball at a professional level even when his high school decided to cut him from the team. One of the main reasons these three people became successful is because they all believed they were destined for success. We are all destined for success, but we only get to be successful when we believe in our destiny and stay persistent.
Belief in your ability to succeed gives you motivation similar to that of your vision. Believing in yourself will result in you getting more accomplished and giving yourself higher standards. You don't get to accidentally lead the stampede. Instead, you need to believe in yourself, your idea, and your products right from the start and carry that mindset straight to the finish line.

**The Dream Big Or Go Home Mentality**
It's the harsh truth that many people ignore. The successful people in any niche dreamed big. In fact, one of my tag lines at the end of all of my YouTube videos is to dream big. Dreaming big results in over 100,000 Twitter followers. Dreaming big turns an online yearbook into a multibillion

dollar social network, the one we call Facebook. Dreaming big turns a product that was created in a garage into a multibillion dollar business, the one we call Apple. Dreaming big turns an online bookstore with 1 employee into the multibillion dollar shopping site that we call Amazon. Dreaming big allows a big idea to stem from a business falling apart. That big idea is now called Twitter. In order to create these powerful businesses, the entrepreneurs responsible for these businesses dreamed big. Dreaming big meant envisioning a successful business when the first Mac was made in Steve Jobs' garage. Dreaming big meant being able to see that selling books and keeping the idea alive would allow Amazon to lead the world in ecommerce.

Going home is a lot easier than dreaming big. Going home is the common road to take. However, the common, easy road is not necessarily the best of roads to take. Taking the easy road does result in less work and a wage, but the treasure chest is only at the end of the challenging road. People who take the easier roads by giving themselves the easier goals don't get to lead the stampede. They watch the leaders from the sidelines. The people who are leading their stampedes are the ones who take the more challenging roads and give themselves the more challenging goals.

We need to embrace the truth that these are the only two options. There is no in between. Persistence allows you to go from the ordinary to the extraordinary, but there is nothing between those two terms. You can either be ordinary or extraordinary. The people who tell themselves there is an "in-between" option are just settling for ordinary. The "in-between" mindset cheats the persistence system. The people who think they are "in-between" are the ones who don't get to lead the stampede. There is a middle of the stampede, but the middle of the stampede is different from the "in-between" mindset. The middle of the stampede represents all of the people who are really close to leading the stampede which does not mean "in-between." The people in the middle of the stampede are only there because the people in the front are always hard to catch. People who have the "in-between" mindset believe they are sandwiched in and progress will be difficult. This mindset promotes stopping and does everything it can to prevent someone from going the extra mile. The people in the middle of the stampede are very close to the front while people with the "in-between" mindset are really in the back of the stampede.

## Have The Vision
A vision is essential for many reasons. One of those reasons is that having a vision gives you a standard to reach. By giving yourself weekly, monthly, and yearly visions, you will be able to get more done.
When a certain situation looks bleak--whether that means getting the 1 star review or a product falls apart during the development process--you need to look back at your vision in order to stay motivated. That motivation will give you the persistence you need to cross the finish line.

The mistake too many people make is letting all of the difficulties get under their skin. Those difficulties result in less work getting done and more time being spent on the couch. The vision will keep you off the couch and give you something to strive for. With a deadline for your vision, you will give yourself a better reason to be productive.

## Persistence Can Be Acquired Over Time

If you do not have persistence now, it is possible to acquire persistence over time. In fact, all skills are learnable if you are willing to put in the time and effort. If you do not have persistence, it will take time to develop it, but any person has the ability to develop persistence. Persistence is what allows the people in the middle of the stampede to lead the stampede later on. Persistence allows people to face rejections more times than they count and still end up becoming very successful. Persistence is something we should all strive for and improve upon, whether we have a lot of persistence or if that persistence needs some work.

## Google Finally Nails It With Google+

When we think of Google's social network, we think of Google+. However, Google experimented with numerous social networks before coming up with Google+. They all flopped, and it looked since Google+ was not popular during its first look, it looked as if Google+ would be another flop. After creating products  and tools such as Google+ Hangouts that revolved around having a Google+ account and updating the social network, Google+ was

168

finally able to become a powerful social network. Then, Google's search engines gave people with Google+ an exclusive edge. More people wanted that edge, and as a result, more people went to Google+. As it became popular, friends told their friends about Google+. The products and SEO advantage that came with Google+ were no longer a deciding factor towards getting more users. People created accounts on Google+ and learned about the Google+ advantage later on. Social media experts began to use and recommend Google+. The social network that looked as if it would fail ended up becoming a commonly used word in blog posts, forums, and through word of mouth. Now Google+ is one of the largest social networks on the web. After many trails and errors, Google finally came out with a powerful social network. Google's persistence throughout the entire process allowed Google+ to thrive. If Google gave up on Google+, Google would have just experimented with another social network later on. Instead of giving up, Google made innovations to Google+ that allowed it to become a different kind of social network.

# The Ability To Make Connections

Making connections is a very important factor that will help you lead the stampede of your niche. Connections may result in you learning more about your niche, gaining more customers, and getting more opportunities. There are numerous ways to connect with other people in your niche. Some of these connections may start off as simple as saying hi to each other on Twitter. One of the results down the line could be that person inviting you to speak at their event.

## Have A Business Card With You At All Times

You never know where or when connections will happen. Some connections will happen on social media while others will happen in person. When you connect with someone in person, it helps to have your business card with you so you can give it to that person before your conversation comes to a close. Some people believe business cards are 'a thing of the past' but they are still exchanged today. There are many networking events will encourage speakers and participants to exchange contact information with each other. Getting someone's contact information makes it possible for the connection to build after a networking event.

Connections in person will either work flawlessly or be horrendous. In this sense, horrendous simply means that the connection you made was broken because you and the person you connected with had no way of contacting each other. You don't know that person's social networks and they don't know about yours. Having a business card with you at all times will solve the problem.

**How To Make A Good Business Card**
While having a business card is important, it is also important to have an effective business card. You want the recipient to easily identify your social networks and what you and your business do on the front of the business card. One of the mistakes people make is having information on both the front and the back of the business card. Most people who receive a business card do not bother looking at the back of the business card. That means most people will not even know about the information you put at the back of your business card. Putting your information on the back of the card may even be an inconvenience since some people take quick notes on the back of a business card.

In addition to avoiding the back of the business card, you should also avoid having too much text on the business card. More text makes a business card harder to read, and that is why having images and a logo on your business card is extremely important. An image pops out at us compared to the text in a book. Instead of writing the links or the usernames for your social networks, have pictures of the social media icons at the top right and top left of your business card. At the center of the business card should be your business' logo or a picture of you with a short description. In that short description should be your email address because email is the best way of contacting potential customers. Have as few words as possible for the description and on the business card in general. You should aim to have less than 10 words on a personal business card and less than 20 words on the business card for your brand. Additionally, you should provide your cell phone number or your business' phone number so people have another option to communicate with you.

**Business Card Etiquette**
There is an etiquette towards giving out a business card. At a grocery store, people are not expecting to be handed a business card. At a business expo, people expect to be given many business cards, but shoving business cards in front of people's faces is not the right way to build a strong connection.
The best way to give out a business card is by having a long conversation with the person first. While the conversation is developing, decide whether or not the person you are talking to could be a potential customer or someone who would promote you in any way. It is important to remember that a potential customer is someone who would want to buy and could benefit from your product, not someone with a full wallet. If you decide the person is not the type of person who would be interested in your business or buy your products, you should only give that person your business card if he offer you his business card or expects to be given a business card. If he is not expecting a business card, then there is no need to give that person your business card.

If you decide the person you are talking to is a potential customer or brings another benefit to the table, give that person your business card as the conversation comes to an end. Be sure to tell the person to contact you through your email so you can stay in touch. The better your conversation was with that person, the more likely that person is to send you an email. If the person decides to email you, be sure to follow up with that person as soon as possible. The quicker you follow up with that person, the more likely that person is to remember who you are.

In the end, when it comes to distributing business cards, it's not about how many hands your business cards wind up in. It's about how many potential customers get your business card.

## Using Social Media To Build Connections

Social media has allowed people who no one knew become well-known experts of their niches. The reason that many unknown people became well-known through social media was because they were able to make many connections. Some of these connections gave them the chance to appear in popular magazines, websites, and newspapers such as *Forbes*, *The Huffington Post*, and others.

There are many social networks to choose from. While some of the rules are different--such as the character count, whether a picture is mandatory in a post or not, and other factors--there are many rules that apply to all of the social networks. All social networks require you to have conversations with other people in order to build quality connections. Social media is the best tool to build connections because it is a free platform with millions of users that you can connect with. You may not be able to connect all of the millions of people who use social media, but imagine how different your business would be if you connected with 100 people. Then, imagine how different your business would be if you connected with 1,000 people. Connecting with people on social media can also result in more sales. In fact, many of the people who bought and reviewed my book *How To Be Successful On Twitter* were following me on Twitter before they bought and reviewed the book.

You don't need a digital product to get more sales. Inspyr Socks is a business that sells socks with motivational messages such as "Never Give Up," "Believe, Achieve," and "Think It, Be It." Inspyr Socks uses social media to interact with its audience and promote its products along the way. The genius behind their marketing is that when they use social media, they will post motivational messages on Twitter and Facebook while promoting their socks. Inspyr Socks also uses social media to get in contact with people and organizations who want to distribute Inspyr Socks to other people. Since the socks are cool (I should be able to look at my socks and feel motivated), and they grab attention (look at all of those bright colors and motivational messages), Inspyr Socks brings in more sales as more people see them. Inspyr Socks may not have a gigantic social media audience, but they know how to effectively use social media and interact with their community.

On any social network, it is important to post new content consistently and frequently. If you are inconsistent with posting your content, your followers will not know when you will produce new content. If you are consistent with your posts but only send out 1 post on your social networks every day, your followers are not going to see you as often on their newsfeeds. When I decided to tweet every 30 minutes instead of every hour, I saw better results. When I decided to tweet every 20 minutes, my results got even better. Increasing my consistency and frequency allowed me to see better results. One of the results was that more people started to read my blog. As more people read my blog posts, they shared my blog posts on their social networks and my audience grew. When more people started sharing my blog posts, I started to gain more Twitter followers, make more connections (that were also extremely valuable), get more sales, and get more blog subscribers. On Twitter and other social networks, it is important to show up on as many people's feeds as frequently as possible.

## How To Get More Engagement
## On Your Social Networks

In order to build more connections using your social networks, you need to increase the engagement you get on your social networks. There are numerous ways to get more engagement with your social networks.

One of the simplest methods to getting more engagement on your social networks is by asking a question. When I decided to ask people what their favorite book was, 8 people replied to the tweet, and many of those responses turned into lengthy conversations. My followers and I were able to add new books to our reading lists, and I got to interact with 8 other people.

Another way to engage with your followers is by having long conversations with those followers. In order to engage with your followers in long conversations, you need to reply to your followers when they mention you as soon as possible. There is a difference between responding to someone within a few hours and responding to someone within a few days. Responding to a follower within a few hours will give that follower a way to add on to the conversation quicker. Our attention spans are short, and if you do not continue a conversation with one of your followers for several days, that follower may forget that the conversation took place. You should see who mentioned you on social media at least three times every day: in the morning, the afternoon, and in the evening. By checking in three times every day, you will be able to continue conversations for a longer period of time. If no one mentions you within that timeframe, get involved in someone else's conversation or start a conversation with another person. You should always be interacting on social media.

**Tweeting At 2 am**

When I was starting to take social media seriously, I decided that I would tweet once an hour from 9 am to 9 pm. The reason I stopped at 9 pm was that I could not imagine who could possibly be on Twitter after that time. 10 pm seemed late to send out a tweet, but 2 am seemed like an absurd time to send out a tweet. A common mistake is that people forget that there are different time zones in the world. If it is 9 pm in New York, then it is 6 pm in California. There are bigger time gaps in other countries. 2 am in your time zone may be the afternoon in someone else's time zone.

That's why I now tweet multiple times every hour 24/7 for 365 days. By tweeting at this frequency, I am able to reach out to more people who live in different time zones. The hours that you would never be awake are the hours when some people are eating breakfast and looking at their timelines on their social networks. Not sending out as many tweets is the easier option, but the easier option is not necessarily the better of the two. Since there are different timezones throughout the world, it is important for you to send out tweets throughout the day so you can build an international audience. However, if most of your customers are on the East Coast, only send tweets at reasonable hours for that timezone.

**Building More Connections With Your Blog**

My blog saw a big increase in traffic immediately after I tweeted about it more often on Twitter. I was also able to set up my blog at that time to build more connections with my visitors. The mistake a lot of bloggers make is not preparing for the day they see a big increase in visitors. Once you get many people to visit your blog, you want them to stick around.

The four best ways to get more visitors to stay on your blog is by getting them to subscribe, getting them to comment on your blog posts, getting them to contact you via email, and constantly publishing quality content. All four of these factors are essential towards building stronger connections with your visitors. Whether your blog is getting thousands of visitors every day or a few visitors every week, your blog needs to be prepared for a big increase in traffic.

**How The Four Factors Work Together**
The four factors: (1) constantly publishing quality content, (2) getting visitors to subscribe, (3) getting people to comment on your blog posts, and (4) getting them to contact you via email, work together towards allowing you to interact with more of your visitors while providing them with more value. Some of these visitors may even decide to visit your blog every day. The most important factor is the quality content. The content of your blog is a crucial factor of whether or not a visitor subscribes to your blog. The content of your blog also has the potential to encourage comments. People who are subscribed to your blog are also more likely to leave comments. When people visit your blog for the first time and see a lot of interaction (the comments), they will decide to comment as well. If a visitor

not subscribed to your blog leaves a comment, that visitor may be more likely to subscribe to your blog. As people subscribe to your blog, leave comments, and read your content, some will contact you. Some people will contact you with questions while others will contact you with opportunities. I have been interviewed several times because people were able to contact me through my blog. Even if your blog is not getting a lot of visitors now, you should have your blog well prepared for the day it gets a dramatic rise in visitors (because with persistence, any blogger can make it big). No matter what you are selling, whether it be a digital product or a physical product, a blog is a great way to grow an audience and increase your sales.

**Writing Quality Content**
Writing quality content will make people stay on your blog for a longer period of time. The more time someone spends on your blog, the more likely that person is to comment on one of your blog posts and subscribe to your blog. Quality content will also establish you as an expert who knows a lot about the niche. It is also the type of content that is more likely to spread. No matter how much you promote a low quality blog post, that low quality blog post is not going to get shared many times. Quality content is the starting point towards success.

There are some disputes of who is the king. Some people say that the content is king while other people say that traffic is king. It seems as if many aspects of a successful blog are fighting for one crown. The secret is that quality content and traffic are both needed. You need quality content in order to get people to stay on your blog and you need good traffic to get people to visit your blog in the first place. Quality content gives you credibility, and you will need to have credibility in order to lead the stampede.

## Getting People To Subscribe To Your Blog

The people who are subscribed to your blog are the ones who visit your blog multiple times every week. If they are not visiting your blog, most of the subscribers are reading the emails you send them about your blog posts. This results in more people knowing about your presence on the web.

Subscribers are your most loyal fans, and some subscribers eventually become customers. While some subscribers will buy your products right away, others may decide to buy your products months or even years later. Quality content is not the only factor that decides how many people will subscribe to your blog. Another factor that goes into how many subscribers you get is whether or not it is easy for someone to subscribe to your blog. Do visitors have to search for the subscription box, or can they simply enter their email address in a subscription box that is easy to see? Making the subscription box bigger so that more people can see it. A tiny subscription box gets less attention, and as a result, less subscribers.

Another great way to get more blog subscribers is by offering something free that is exclusive to your blog subscribers. What can you give away for free? The best thing to do is to turn your knowledge into a digital free prize such as a video, PDF, or report. I offer a free video about Mastering Pinterest and other goodies while other people offer a PDF or report. As long as you are giving something of value to all of the people who subscribe to your blog, you will entice more people to subscribe to your blog. Give your new visitors an incentive to subscribe to your blog. After the new visitor subscribes to your blog, gets the free product, and reads some of your blog posts, they will not have to be given an incentive to read your blog posts. The content you publish will be the incentive.

**Keep Your Visitors On Your Blog As Long As Possible**
The problem with advertisements is that they take up a lot of space and encourage people to leave your blog. That is why my blog does not have advertisements. By keeping someone on your blog for a long period of time, that person is more likely to subscribe. There are numerous tactics to increase the amount of time people visit your blog such as adding links to older blog posts in your new blog posts, and linking to the pages on your blog. The longer someone stays on your blog, the more likely that person is to subscribe to your blog and become a connection.

**Connecting With Your Subscribers Via Email**
After you get the subscriber, it is important to interact with that subscriber. Since you had all of your subscribers enter their email address, you have a way to connect with them.

The automated emails will do their job of thanking someone, offering the free product, and asking the person to verify their email address. However, automated emails are not going to lead to strong connections.

In order to build stronger connections, you need to contact your subscribers manually. The biggest benefit this has is that the subscriber is more likely to stick around. When a subscriber gets contacted by the blogger, that makes the subscriber feel special. You want all of your subscribers to feel special about the decision they made (subscribing to your blog). You do that by contacting them via email and building stronger connections.

In your email, start off by thanking the person for subscribing to your blog. It is important to include the name of your blog because most of your subscribers are subscribed to other blogs as well. Providing the name of your blog will allow your subscribers to remember who you are. When thanking the person for subscribing to your blog, ask them what questions they have about your niche. If any of your subscribers emails you with a question, answer it as soon as possible. Not only does this allow you to build strong connections with your subscribers, but you will also be able to come up with new ideas for blog posts. By answering many common questions, you can eventually create an FAQ page on your blog. This will result in a higher quality blog and encourage more people to subscribe to your blog.

Connecting to your subscribers via email will allow you to build connections that result in new customers. After reading a few of your blog posts and having a conversation with you via email, some of your subscribers will buy your products. Instead of focusing on building the list, focus on the list that you already have. Then, more people will gradually get added to the list as they subscribe to your blog.

**Getting More People To Comment On Your Blog**
Comments on your blog show activity. In most cases, the blog posts with the most comments are also the most popular ones. A blog post with 100 comments will most likely get more visitors than a blog post with 5 comments. In addition, having some comments on your blog posts will encourage more people to leave additional comments. The amount of comments you get on your blog posts depends on the size of your audience. A small audience results in few comments while a large audience results in many comments. However, there are ways to get more people to comment on your blog. You do not need to be getting 100,000 daily visitors before you see comments on your blog.
One way to get more comments on your blog is by writing the type of content that encourages comments. Opinion-based, controversial, and informative, are some of the types of content that get more comments. An example of this is saying that Twitter is better than Facebook. Some people will agree that Twitter is better while other people will believe that Facebook is better. Regardless of who likes which social network better, you will get more comments on

your blog. Existing comments will encourage new visitors to leave their own comments as well.

Another way to get more comments is by asking questions throughout the blog post. Asking questions encourages a conversation to build, and at the end of your blog post, do not be afraid to ask for the comment. When you ask for a comment, you need to word it in a proper way that encourages the visitor to leave a comment. Saying, "Please comment below" is not encouraging. Saying, "Please share your thoughts and insights below" is a more encouraging approach to ask for comments. I include this at the end of many of my blog posts, and these are the blog posts that also happen to get the most comments.

**Go To Events In Your Area**
A great way to connect with your target audience is by going to events in your area where people in your targeted audience meet. At an event about social media, the audience at the event wants to learn more about social media. This kind of audience would be my targeted audience. If there is an event in your area related to your expertise, go to it. Not only will you learn more about your niche, but you will also connect with likeminded people. Meetup is a great tool to see which events are happening near you. Not only do you get to search for events happening near you, but you can also search for MeetUps based on certain topics. If you want to go to a MeetUp about fitness, MeetUp will show you all of the events happening near by that are about fitness.

MeetUp is also the perfect tool for you if you want to organize an event related to your expertise. MeetUp allows you to identify the location and get people to pay for tickets online. If you secure a building for your event, MeetUp is a great place to promote that event. Regardless of whether you use MeetUp to find events near you or promote your own event, it is a great way to connect with the people who want your expertise.

# Credibility

Having credibility will allow you to establish yourself as an expert of your niche. Anyone can claim to be an expert. If I wanted to claim I am a fashion expert, all I would have to do is write "fashion expert" for my Twitter bio. Then, people would believe I am an expert in fashion. I am not an expert in fashion which is why that is not in my bio.

In order to be an expert, you need to have credibility and know about your niche. Saying you are an expert is not enough to be an expert. The expert with 100,000 followers who got featured in *Forbes* has a lot of credibility. The expert with 100 followers who has not been featured anywhere does not have as much credibility.

You may be wondering how we define a credible individual. Your expertise, media exposure, and customer testimonials are crucial towards good credibility. One factor that comes into play is big numbers. This thinking process results in a common mistake: buying fake followers. Buying fake followers has turned into a multimillion dollar business, but buying these fake followers does not necessarily result in more retweets or conversations. In order to be credible, those followers need to be real. TwitterAudit has made it very easy to catch people who buy fake followers. Not only does getting caught taint the credibility of having a big following, but it also taints all of your credibility. Only real, big numbers mean anything towards credibility.

The person with 100,000 real followers has a lot of credibility. However, those real numbers are not the only way to build credibility. Building credibility takes the form of appearing in numerous places, posting valuable content, having a product, and a variety of other ways as well. Credibility is something that all leaders in the stampede have.

## How To Get More People To Write About You

Some people have not been written about at all while others have been featured on *Forbes*, *The Huffington Post*, and hundreds of other places as well. There are several factors that go into the number of people who write about you. However, most people are not given the proper knowledge to get more people to write about them.

The number of people who write about you depends on how popular you are. Many people write about the best athletes. There are many articles written about Mariano Rivera, Michael Jordan, Usain Bolt, Tom Brady, and the other big-time athletes. Whether retired or not, these athletes get a lot of attention for being the best at what they do. In addition, millions of people are watching the athletes do what they are good at on TV or at a stadium.

Getting more people to write about you all comes down to getting more attention. How are you getting out there? How are you getting more people to know about you? These are complicated questions to answer for the average entrepreneur, but reaching media outlets (even the big ones like ABC) is not as hard as it sounds.

**Getting Free PR Is Easier Than Ever**
HARO (Help A Reporter Out) has made it a lot easier to get free PR. What originally started as a Facebook group in 2008 has evolved into a powerful way for journalists to connect with people with expertise in certain areas. Some of the media outlets are anonymous while other media outlets are huge. I'm talking about NBC, *Forbes*, CBS, and more!

HARO sends out three emails every day from Monday to Friday with journalists' requests. By submitting your content to these journalists, you have the chance of being featured on a popular blog, magazine, or TV show. Getting featured on one of those places will build your credibility and boost your chances of getting featured on another popular blog, magazine, or TV show.

I recommend submitting a pitch to at least one journalist every day on HARO as long as there is a query that applies to your business. While you may choose to submit to more journalists on some days, submitting to at least one journalist every day will increase the likelihood of you getting featured on a popular blog, magazine, or TV show. When you are crafting your response, be sure to go over the top. If someone asks for one tip, give that person three tips. That way, the journalists will have more tips to choose from. If the journalist does not like your first tip, there are two tips to go. The journalist may decide that the third tip you provide is worth being featured. In the same example, if you only give the journalist your first tip, you won't get featured on the popular blog, magazine, or TV show.

When you are responding to a query, tell the journalist about your credibility. Do you have a blog about the same topic? Do you have a big following on one of your social networks? Do you have a product? Be sure to tell the journalist about your own credibility first. This will give the journalist a stronger reason to write about you. Then, when that journalist writes about you (let's say the journalist is from *Huffington Post*), you will be able to say you were featured on the *Huffington Post* in your future HARO submissions. HARO has made it easier for experts to connect with journalists and reach a larger audience. Reaching this larger audience also results in more credibility.

**Have A Remarkable (But True) Story**
Chances are you have a remarkable story. There are many people who undermine their accomplishments or success and consider it as ordinary. However, there is something remarkable about what you have done, and you can turn that into a true story. We know about many rags to riches stories, and the term became popular because they are remarkable stories. Steve Jobs dropping out of college because he could not afford it is an example of a remarkable story. He went on to create Apple, the multibillion dollar business that we all know very well. Rowling's story is incredible because she was poor when she wrote the first Harry Potter book.
The only problem with these kinds of remarkable stories is that most people feel the need to have a similar experience

in order to have a remarkable story. You do not need to go from rags to riches to have a remarkable story. You can have persistence, take many risks, learn five years of material in one year, or do something else in order to have a remarkable story.

The biggest benefit of having a remarkable story is that people will remember you because of that story. When I think of Dr. Seuss, I think of a children's book author who got rejected more than two dozen times. When I think of Seth Godin, I think of a bestselling author who once got fired by his publisher but didn't give in. There are many remarkable stories out there, and chances are you have your own remarkable story. When you tell journalists your remarkable story, they are more likely to write about you. You may have made a certain amount of money in a few months. You may be a teenager (or you know some teenagers). You may be a stay at home parent who decided to create a strong income by creating your own business. We all have remarkable stories. We just need to let other people know about them.

### How To Get People To Know
### About Your Remarkable Story

The people who are leading their stampedes do not hesitate to let people know about their remarkable stories. Jeremy Schoemaker is another story of rags to riches. He goes in great detail of his transformation on his blog, a magazine wrote how he went from zero figures to eight figures, and he even wrote a book about his remarkable story. He has given away copies of his book for free on his blog before. He has given away a free training course worth close to $200 for people who bought his book when it became a bestseller. He also mentioned that during that time, any new customers who bought the book would also get the free training course. Jeremy Schoemaker basically implemented several tactics to get more people to know about his remarkable story. As a result, there are close to (or slightly over) 100 visitors on his blog at any given moment in real time. His blog does pump out good content, but people simply cannot forget about the Shoemoney blog because of Jeremy's remarkable (but true) story.

The easiest way to let people know about your remarkable story is by writing a lengthy About Me page on your blog with your remarkable story. The About Me page could be paragraphs long. The more you tell your readers, the better. Just be sure to grab their attention within the first paragraph so those people will be more likely to read your entire story. The About Me page is a summarized version of your story, but it is by no means a brief one. Then, tell your remarkable story to journalists so they have an extra reason to feature you on a popular blog, magazine, or TV show. After you gain a big following, write an entire book about your story. Now that people are amazed by your story, they will decide to buy your book so they can learn more about your story. The book should contain the smallest details about your remarkable story, and the better you write the book, the less likely people are to forget about you. In fact, I'm sure some of them will be thinking about your remarkable story for days, weeks, months, or even years. You can become a role model for others. These people will easily subscribe to your blog, buy your other products, and your credibility will soar. At this point, you will be at the front of the stampede you are in.

**Guest Blogging**
In the beginning, your blog will not get thousands of daily visitors. It took more than a day to build Rome, and it also takes more than a day to get thousands of daily visitors on your blog. However, there are already blogs on the web that are getting thousands of daily visitors, and some of those blogs have opportunities for guest bloggers.
Guest blogging is an easy way to put your content in front of thousands of people. Although it is important to have your own blog and publish new content on it often, becoming a guest blogger will allow you to put your content in front of a larger audience. Being able to say that you are a guest blogger will show people that your content is good enough to get showcased on other blogs. Being a guest blogger on Social Media Today means your content is good enough to get your content on Social Media Today. Being a contributor on the *Huffington Post* means you are good enough to have been able to contribute to the *Huffington Post*. When you write on a blog that is credible, you gain credibility. Social Media Today is a very credible blog. Being a guest blogger on Social Media Today would give you more credibility. When choosing which guest blogs to write for, choose the ones that are very credible in your niche. A

sports guest blog is not the right place to write about getting more Twitter followers, but a social media guest blog is the perfect place to write about getting more Twitter followers. Choosing your niche will allow you to get credibility from writing on guest blogs that your target audience can appreciate.

Consistently guest blogging will be helpful towards spreading your remarkable story. People may not look at your bio when they see your first guest post, but trust comes from being seen frequently. If someone reads and likes 10 of your guest posts, that person may decide to read your bio. Then, they read your remarkable story and your list of accomplishments. Some of the people who read your remarkable story will have their minds wrapped around your story for a long period of time.

**How Having A Product Builds Credibility**

Having a product is essential towards building credibility. It seems as if all of the successful entrepreneurs and experts have a bestselling book or a training course. It's not a coincidence. Having a product boosts credibility by a landslide. Content marketing allows other people to get a taste of what you are about and what you offer. The product is (hopefully) more valuable than the content you offer for free. After reading your free content, some readers will end up buying the product.

Having a product simply shows you are good enough to create a product. If the product brings in a good income, it simply shows that you are good enough to create a product that brings in a strong income. Being good enough to do those things will impress many people who are trying to learn what you teach. In addition, having a product will make people see you as a smart person who knows more about your niche than the average person in your niche. To put it in simple terms, having a product puts you above 99% of the people in your niche who have not created a product yet. In addition, having a product will make people view you as an expert in your niche. As you create more products, you will learn more about your niche and become smarter.

## Does Any Product Do The Job?

That depends on how valuable the product is. The more valuable your product is, the more of an expert that product will make you look like. A professional training course makes the trainer look like an expert. An unprofessional training course still makes the trainer look like an expert because he has a product. However, the unprofessional training course does not do a good job at encouraging people to buy more of your products. Whether you write a book or you create a training course, the quality of the product is the decisive factor of how many people see you as an expert, and how close you are to the front of the stampede.

## Keeping Credibility

Once you get credibility, it is important to retain that credibility for as long as you can. In addition, it is important to build on the credibility that we have already mustered. In order to keep your credibility, you need to remain consistent. If you are credible for giving good home tips on your blog, you need to consistently publish blog posts in order to keep the credibility. If you do not publish blog posts and leave the blog inactive, the credibility will go away. After leaders of stampedes gain credibility, they stay consistent in order to keep that credibility. That's one of the reasons why consistency is a key element to leading the stampede. Not only is consistency key towards becoming a leader, but it is also key towards keeping the credibility you have.

**Gaining Credibility Becomes Easier Over Time**
Gaining credibility involves going one step at a time. As your credibility builds, it will be easier for you to gain more credibility. If you get featured in the *Associated Press*, chances are other big media outlets will mention you. News that reaches the *Associated Press* also reaches other big media outlets such as ABC, national newspapers, and more.
If you choose to gain credibility by doing what you love, the process of gaining credibility will be made a lot easier. Your expertise and content marketing give you some of the credibility, and as more people hear about you (and as you submit more responses to HARO), big media outlets start to pay attention. Gaining credibility is not the easiest thing to do, but gaining credibility is not the hardest thing to do either. It just takes time and commitment.

# The Desire To Become Successful

Out of all of the characteristics, this one may seem like the easiest to follow. We all want to become the person with the $1 million mansion with an indoor track (as a track runner, that's what I would want anyway). However, the desire to be successful means being willing to put in the work in order to become successful even after the realization that success does not come easy.

It's easy to want success. Everyone wants to be successful. However, desiring success in such a way that you are committed to accomplishing all of the tasks in front of you is an essential characteristic to have in order to lead the stampede. The desire to be successful is your need to gain a local, regional, or international impact on the world.

## There Are No Accidents

People did not become successful because of accidents. People became successful because they had a strong desire for success in the first place. You don't end up becoming the CEO by accident. You don't end up creating a multimillion dollar product by accident.

Many people keep on believing that they will accidentally find success. This thinking process gives these people no control of how and when they become successful. In addition, these people end up not becoming successful because they have no course of direction.

The leaders of the stampede do not acquire their spots by accident. People who win races do not win by accident. Products and services do not accidentally end up making thousands of sales. By realizing that there are no accidents or easy shortcuts, and by looking at the work ahead, you will be able to acquire a desire for success.

## You Are Destined To Succeed
It's okay to think that way. There is nothing egotistical about that (unless you tell everyone around you about your destined success). This is the mindset I used to get to where I am today, and I continue to have this thought in my mindset to this day. Believing that you are destined for success will allow you to go further and move up in your stampede.

## Have Faith In Yourself
Your greatest ally or your greatest enemy is who you see when you look in the mirror. In order to see yourself as your own greatest ally, you need to have faith in yourself. You need to believe in your products and services. You need to believe that one day your product will end up making thousands of sales after countless hours of work. You need to have faith in yourself in order to succeed.

## The Desire To Learn More About Your Niche
In order to become the leader of your stampede, you need to learn more about your niche. The most common pitfall is that people think they know everything about the niche they are in. Although it is good to believe in yourself and be confident, being overconfident can hinder growth.

It is impossible to know everything about a single niche, but it is important to get as close as possible to knowing everything about your niche. These are some of the different things you can use to learn more about your niche.

1. **Blog posts related to your niche**. Blog posts are free resources on the web to learn a lot about your niche. If you happen to hunger for knowledge related to digital marketing, my blog www.marcguberti.com provides over one thousand free digital marketing articles.

2. **Books related to your niche**. Although books are not free, they provide a lot of information (depending on the book you read). The right books are the ones that discuss powerful methods and introduces ones that you have not heard of or taken seriously. Buying this book shows me that you want to learn how to take charge and be the leader of your niche.

3. **YouTube videos related to your niche**. YouTube is a free way to gain access to a lot of information about your niche. If you subscribe to 10 channels related to your niche and watch all of the videos on those channels, you are going to learn a lot from them.

4. **Training courses and membership sites**. Most training courses and membership sites provide more information and insights than individual YouTube videos. Good training courses and membership sites give you a clear path to take and gives you a sense of direction. Instead of having a slight understanding of many skills, you are given what you need to master the most important skills in your niche. You can browse through some free training

courses on the web related to your niche to see what they are made of before you consider paying for a more advanced training course.

## How Dedicated Are You?

Taking the time to learn more about your niche shows that you are dedicated. Taking the time to put in the hard work shows that you are dedicated. Taking the time to do other activities revolving around your niche will show your clients how dedicated you are to giving them the best quality.

In order to be a leader, you need to have dedication, and there's no way around this one. The amount of dedication you have relates to your desire to become successful. Everyone wants success, but when you have a strong desire to become successful, you eventually become dedicated. The amount of dedication you have is also related to how much you love what you do. That is the next characteristic of people who lead their stampedes.

# The Love For What You Do

In order to become a leader in your niche, you need to have a strong passion for that niche. Putting on a baseball cap and saying you are going to be a baseball player will not work if you do not like the sport. Instead of choosing something for the income, choose to do what you love to do and turn that into a strong income. Instead of thinking of work as a drag, think of work as something fun and worth doing. If you do what you love, you will not work a single day in your life. In addition, putting in more hours will become easier since you are not working--you are simply doing what you love.

## What Makes A Good Author

A good author is not necessarily someone who picks up the pen and starts writing. A good author is someone who loves writing, reads books, and enjoys the journey that his/her book is taking. The good authors are the ones who love to write. The authors that few people know about are the ones who do not like to write as much. Do not publish a book just to say that you wrote a book. Publish a book because you love writing about a certain topic and sharing it with the world.

## The Incredible Journey Of A Man Who Created Multiple Businesses Based On What He Loves To Do

Craig Wolfe has started multiple businesses, and not only did they end up becoming successful, but Craig started businesses that revolved around the things that he loves to do. Craig has a great appreciation for artwork, and that appreciation for artwork turned into a business. After a friend lent him $500, Craig was able to use that $500 to become the largest publisher of artwork from television commercials. Craig created the first ever animation art lines for Coca-Cola, Annheuser-Bush, M&M, and others as well. Not only did Craig love what he did, but this was also a small innovation. None of these Fortune 500 companies had any idea that they could sell the artwork from their commercials just like Disney, and Craig showed them the way (and made decent money from it too).

This business alone is a big accomplishment, but Craig decided to make another small innovation. This small innovation involved rubber ducks and celebrities. The result was CelebriDucks, a multimillion dollar business in which the products are rubber ducks modeled after celebrities. Some of the rubber duck celebrities are the greatest icons of film, music history, and sports. CelebriDucks was voted as one of the Top 100 Gifts by Entertainment Weekly and featured on hundreds of TV shows, magazines, and newspapers including *The Tonight Show*. Just to give you an idea of the diversity of the celebrity rubber ducks, you can have a line of four rubber ducks that look like Barack Obama, Jesus, Shakespeare, and Gene Simmons. Although CelebriDucks was made in America, the business eventually went overseas in order to save money. However, when CelebriDucks became a big success, Craig decided to take another big step by addressing the importance of bringing jobs back to America. He was tired of seeing the entire country outsourced, and his solution was to bring the CelebriDucks business back to America. Now, CelebriDucks is the only rubber duck business in which the rubber ducks are made from start to finish in America. The only reason some of the CelebriDucks business is still overseas is because people who are overseas want discounts for the celebrity rubber ducks. As CelebriDucks continues to grow, some celebrities are asking for personalized rubber ducks.

CelebriDucks certainly put Craig on the map, but he was not done. Craig decided that he needed to create something else. He just launched a new chocolate division which you can see at www.CocoaCanard.com with their Spooning Chocolate, the only dairy and gluten free hot chocolate that can be mixed in a cup of hot water. Craig and his team spent a year trying to figure out how to create the dessert, and now it is the go-to product in its category. After interviewing Craig, he told me that the trick he uses is to do what he loves while being different from everyone else at the same time. Craig has mastered the characteristics that are required to lead a stampede, and that is exactly how Craig was able to create thriving businesses based on the things that he loves to do.

### Houstonian Hotel, Club, & Spa's Public Relations Director Loves What She Does

Houston native Leslie Friedman is able to do what she loves while staying close to home. Leslie is the public relations director for The Houstonian Hotel, Club, & Spa which is a luxurious property in Houston, Texas, with a four-star hotel, 175,000 square foot fitness club, and an award-winning spa. Leslie is able to go to work every day looking forward to help promote hospitality, health, fitness, and relaxation. Leslie shares remarkable stories about individuals and places at the Houstonian Hotel, Club, & Spa to various reporters that range from local to international. Leslie is certainly doing what she loves to do, and the results show. Leslie has won awards for her skills in media relations and has been successful throughout her entire career with media placements and publicity. Leslie has been an important factor towards The Houstonian Hotel, Club, & Spa's success and ultimately allowed it to stand out from the other hotel, club, & spas in Houston.

### Why Journalist Stephen Robert Morse Became A Marketer

Some people pursue their passion to the point where they switch out of their current role in order to go after a new niche. Stephen Robert Morse is no stranger to changing roles in order to pursue a passion. Before becoming a marketer, Stephen was a journalist. Not only was Stephen a journalist, but he was writing for popular magazines and websites such as *Mother Jones*, *The Boston Globe*, *The Atlantic*, *Philadelphia Inquirer*, *The Huffington Post*, and *Fast Company*.

The main reason Stephen stopped focusing most of his time on journalism is because he was fearful about his future. The pay for journalists is small, and Stephen was worried about how he would be able to afford food and a place to sleep. Another reason Stephen stopped focusing most of his time on journalism is because of something one of his high school teachers said. The teacher said that there are three types of people in the world: those who watch things happen, those who make things happen, and those who do not realize that anything has happened. As a journalist, Stephen felt as if he were watching things happen instead of making things happen.

Stephen had always been a marketer, but now that marketing was his priority, it became his profession. Stephen was working day by day as a journalist for MTV and had a fellowship in Entrepreneurial Journalism at the CUNY Grad School of Journalism in New York. Stephen's second job was a freelance journalist for a tech publication. Stephen interviewed Ryan Scott, the VP of Marketing at seamless.com and got along with him very well. Ryan suggested that Stephen could become his copywriter. Stephen did not think anything of it at the time, but everything changed when MTV cut the show that he was working in. Then, the stars aligned. Stephen reached out to Ryan, was interviewed, and got the job.

At that moment, Stephen went into marketing and has worked for many startups ever since. He has advised the marketing teams for Shapeways, Handvaerk, Quirky.com, and others. Stephen has mastered data analytics and stays within a limited startup budget. While some businesses spend money at will, Stephen has to be selective with the way he spends his money. By giving himself a budget,

Stephen is able to be creative with the money that he has. Some of Stephen's budget goes into Google AdWords and other ad exchange platforms. By combining his creativity and quantitative side of marketing, Stephen is able to create excellent email marketing and other ad campaigns. The reason Stephen knows a lot about marketing is because he has a passion for it. This passion for marketing is what encouraged him to focus less of his time on journalism. By pursuing his passion, Stephen was able to bring in more income and have fun at work. Stephen is still a journalist, but now he focuses most of his time on marketing. Now, Stephen gets to make things happen instead of watch them happen.

**Young Entrepreneur Jeet Banerjee Starts Early**
California native Jeet Banerjee knew exactly what he wanted to do when he was in high school (sounds familiar). Jeet started his first business, JB Media Force, as a junior in high school. JB Media Force was a multimedia agency offering web design, web development, online marketing, and mobile development services to businesses of all sizes. JB Media Force grew to a business with over 15 employees, and some of those employees were overseas. Jeet ran this company while going to school before selling it two years later.

At 21 years old, Jeet is a serial entrepreneur, digital marketing consultant, bestselling author, public speaker (also a TEDx Speaker), and change-maker. Jeet has systematized his entire business and now makes over

$250,000 annually. Jeet's bestselling book, *Limitless Thinking* provides people with the solutions for three big obstacles towards starting a business: lack of money, experience, and degrees. Jeet started his business with none of the three. Jeet shares what he has learned as an entrepreneur, scenarios in his journey, and how others can embark on a journey like his. Jeet did not spend any money to build his following on Twitter, and by telling his followers and blog's visitors about *Limitless Thinking*, the book became a bestseller on Amazon within 48 hours.

Another one of Jeet's startup adventures was Statfuse which allows students to enter in their data and see how likely they are to get into a certain university. Jeet created this startup when he was about to graduate high school when he and his business partners were making a bet on whether or not he would get into Harvard. In the end, Jeet never applied to Harvard, but Statfuse allowed them to figure out whether Jeet would have gotten into Harvard or not. Now, Statfuse is a revolutionary platform that is disrupting college admissions. Before sending in a college admission, you are now able to see how likely you are to make it into the school before applying.

Jeet has created several training courses that show startups and entrepreneurs how to be successful. These training courses are packed with content, have received many 5 star reviews, and have been tweeted out over 200 times. Jeet knew what he wanted to do, and his determination allowed him to become successful at a young age.

## NFL Cheerleader Pursues Her Passion
## For Being A Motivational Speaker

Shannon Oleen's family has a strong passion for sports. Her great uncle pitched in the World Series and her mother was an athlete as well. After playing in many sports, Shannon decided in high school that she become a cheerleader. Shannon pursued this dream in high school, college, and afterwards when she got the Head Cheerleading Coaching position at Pembroke Hill High School. Shannon became a Sales and Marketing Recruiter while she was a coach at Pembroke Hill High School. She remained a Sales and Marketing Recruiter for three years when she developed a skill set to help people become happier by helping them find the right job. With all of this going on, Shannon Oleen decided to pursue her passion and try out for the Kansas City Chief's Cheerleader Squad. Shannon did not make it during her first try in 2008, but a year later, after countless practice sessions of preparation, Shannon tried out again and made the team!

What's even more amazing is that the story continues. Shannon remembered that as a teenager, she did not know what she wanted to become in her life. She did not know at the time that cheerleading would be her profession. Shannon also realized that there were still many people in her community who were currently going through the same experience of not knowing their aspirations. Shannon decided to retire from cheerleading in 2011 to become a motivational speaker for young adults. Ever since, Shannon has been empowering thousands of people with the framework needed to accomplish their dreams and thrive. I decided to interview Shannon and ask her about her success. She told me that one of the reasons she became successful was because she never went with the status quo. Shannon would not allow metrics, statistics, and numbers to define what her career would be. Instead, Shannon chose her career based on her passions and is now a highly recognized motivational speaker. You can learn more about Shannon and follow her journey by visiting her website, www.shannonoleen.com.

## Head Of A Major Agency
## Becomes A University Professor

Ron Culp had worked major corporate and agency jobs including being the head of the North American Corporate Practice for Ketchum. After 40 years of doing this, Ron got bored with his job. However, the thought of retiring sounded even more boring for Ron. He kept working at his job and became an adjunct professor at DePaul University in Chicago. Ron was an adjunct for 11 weeks and taught for 3 hours every Tuesday night. Being an adjunct professor at DePaul University opened Ron to a different kind of work. Ron loved the new challenge and the ability to share his professional experiences while continuing to learn more about his niche.

After one stint as an adjunct professor, the dean asked Ron to help find and recruit a professional director of the PR and advertising program at DePaul. Ron was able to find someone for the job, but that person later turned down the job after talking with students who wanted someone with real-world experience. The dean told Ron to find another person for the job and went on to say that the reason Ron did not have the job was because the university could not afford him.

Then, Ron came up with a crazy idea. Ron decided that he should be the professor at DePaul University and work for less pay. Ron frequently gave guest lectures in college settings which made him eager to take the job. Ron mentioned the idea to his wife who was at first not open to the idea. Although he knew he would make less money, Ron knew that he would be happier to take the job. The next day, Ron called the dean, quit his agency job, and became a professor at DePaul University. Although he sacrificed money, he was able to do something that he was passionate about instead of "just showing up." Ron still consults with some public relations clients, but 90% of his time is spent in DePaul University.

Another thing Ron does is write blog posts for his blog that focuses on young people pursuing careers in public relations. Ron got the idea to start his own blog when a group of interns asked him if he ever considered writing a blog. The thought of sharing career tips with a broader group of up-and-coming professionals fascinated Ron. Ron decided to ask the interns to develop a proposal about what the blog might contain and look like. A few days later, three of the interns scheduled time with Ron to make their presentation. After collaboration, Ron and the interns decided to name the blog Culpwrit.com. With his own blog, Ron is now able to reach out to more people on the web. Before Ron became a professor at DePaul University and create a blog, he was working in a job that he considered boring. Ron saw the opportunity to do something that he would love to do. Although Ron sacrificed some of his income to make the transition, Ron was able to get his dream job. Having a dream job will allow you to do that job more effectively. Would you do better at something you can't stand or something that you enjoy? We would all do better at something if we enjoyed it. As a professor at DePaul University with a blog about careers in public relations, Ron definitely enjoys the work that he does.

**Military Veteran Now Does What He Loves**
Chip Bell is a really awesome guy. Chip served in the military during the Vietnam War as a reconnaissance unit commander with the elite 82nd Airborne and had finished at the top of his class at the Army Jungle Survival School in Panama. Through his experiences of protecting the United States from harm, Chip discovered how much he loved training and speaking. After he served in Vietnam, Chip became the Director of Management and Organization Development for Bank of America (at the time, Bank of America was still called NCNB). After a few years of working for NCNB, Chip decided to start his own consulting company, The Chip Bell Group and later on became a part of the Keynote speaker circuit.

The Chip Bell Group, formed in 1980, is a confederation of highly experienced consultants who passionately pursue one core vision which is to help clients become famous by showing those clients how to grow their businesses. All members of the The Chip Bell Group are independent consultants with their own consulting practices. The Chip Bell Group's brand strategy is to consistently do remarkable work on behalf of their clients.

It has been almost 50 years since Chip finished graduate school. Although some of his friends retired from the workforce, Chip shows no signs of retiring. Chip is someone who loves what he does, and the people who are passionate about their work will end up living longer, staying healthier, and finding life as an absolute gift. Chip is someone who does what he loves, and as a result, Chip has been able to live a wonderful and fun-filled life.

## Amy Rodbell Leaves The Status Quo
## To Do What She Always Wanted To Do

When she graduated college, Amy Rodbell pursued various career options working at a variety of jobs from Capitol Hill as a staff assistant to a Georgia congressman to working in government affairs for Coca-Cola. Eventually, Amy retired so she could stay home with her newborn son.

The amount of extra time Amy had allowed her to nurture her newborn son and take more time to think about her true passions and creative pursuits. After identifying her true passions and creative pursuits, Amy started a costume jewelry business called Swell Caroline Costume Jewelry one year after she retired. The Atlanta based business launched their wholesale business through trade shows and is growing in other geographic areas. Most of Swell Caroline Costume Jewelry's customers are preppy customers from the southeast United States who according to the Swell Caroline website are girls sophisticated in taste, though never a snob, and she loves to stand out in a crowd.

Amy founded Swell Caroline Costume Jewelry at the right time. At the time, Pinterest was a new social network that everyone was getting used to. Swell Caroline Costume Jewelry was one of the early players on the new social network and now boasts over 10,000 Pinterest followers. 65% of Swell Caroline Costume Jewelry's website traffic comes directly from Pinterest, and they optimize other social networks (Twitter, Facebook, Instagram, and Google Plus) as well. In the wholesale market, Swell Caroline distributed their channels to smooth out their sales so they did not become dependent on one customer base.

Swell Caroline differentiates from the competition by updating time tested classic designs and developing new designs incorporating bright colors and unexpected elements. Unlike most of its competitors, Swell Caroline does not create costume jewelry based on moment trends. Instead, they create designs that women will wear for years to come. Swell Caroline designs pieces with luxurious elements and high quality findings and looks at the market to identify an affordable price point for her costume jewelry.

Swell Caroline has been featured in *Washington Post*, *CBS*, and other media outlets and continues to grow. Swell Caroline Costume Jewelry can now be found in over 100 retail outlets including retail outlets in NYC and Canada.

### At 17 Years Old, Marc Renson Already
### Knew What He Wanted To Do

Marc Renson likes food, music, and Hollywood. When you walk in and smell the brewing coffee, hear the 80's pop music, see pink feathers, a spinning disco ball and a mural of Madonna, you know you're in Ambition!

Marc has taken his greatest ambitions and created not only a restaurant but he's created his dream! Marc says, "Like attracts like and I like food, music, and Hollywood...welcome to my Ambition!"

Since he was young, Marc has liked music and Hollywood. He especially liked Donna Summer along with the movies 9to5 and Tequila Sunrise. It was Tequila Sunrise that made Marc's soul light up, and at, all of seventeen, made Marc want to own a restaurant.

Fast forward thirteen years later: two guys, one dream and a restaurant named Ambition (taken from Dolly Parton's song, 9to5), was born April 10, 2000.

Marc and his partner purchased a famous landmark tavern which had operated for over 50 years. His partner has marketing expertise and Marc brought with him his personality, a menu and the ambiance right out of a broadway play. Creating an enormous buzz for the restaurant right on their opening day, dining on the grand opening was the Mayor, several local politicians, two TV news stations and three newspapers all showed up wanting to know their secret. Marc said the projected sales for their first day was $120. They grossed $1,200!

Ambition was an immediate success and six months after opening a celebrity entered and that celebrity was 1998 Miss America Kate Shindle. As more celebrities came in over the years, Ambition was dubbed, "Where Hollywood Eats!" Over the years Marc was the personal chef to Bradley Cooper for seven weeks while Bradley filmed the movie The Place Beyond The Pines. Many more celebrities came in including Ryan Gosling, The Cake Boss, KD Lang, Pete Seeger, ESPN founder Bill Rasmussen, Kristen Chenoweth, Barbara Eden and George Hamilton to name a few. Bethenny Frankel also stopped by and made a YouTube video in the Ambition restaurant while on tour. Skinny Girl Day 2 and sent it out to her 1.4 million followers. Marc also feeds the casts and crews of National Broadway touring shows like Jersey Boys, Wicked, Mamma Mia, Book of Mormon and Priscilla Queen of the Desert. His restaurant was featured on broadwayworld.com.

Marc said what contributes to his success is he writes down his goals. Marc said one day he wrote down that he wanted to feed the Boston Pops. He thought the conductor and the pianist would come in. At 8 o'clock that evening, while closing the restaurant, Marc said he received a phone call from the Boston Pops, asking if they could all be fed after one of their shows. Seventy entrees had to be prepared in two hours. Marc said his early idol Donna Summer taught him to be careful for what you wish for!

When I asked Marc about his challenges he said there were many challenges throughout his journey. Some of the challenges Marc faced were employee theft, rising taxes, competition, the city's revitalization construction, the 2008 recession which impacted Ambition for almost two years, and a small fire in the kitchen. Marc added with a laugh, "And crazy customers!" Marc said all of the challenges he went through did not get him down. He decided to write a tell-all book about his journey. His book, *Is The Coffee Fresh?* was picked up by a national publisher in 2011. A humorous journey of what people do, say, and steal from Ambition.

Marc has been very successful over the years. During the interview Marc said, "Money doesn't bring happiness, doing what you love brings happiness!" Marc said that the definition of success is a personal opinion. We all define success differently. But at the end of the day, true success is doing what you love to do. We all have to work, everybody has to work! Yes, even Paris Hilton and Kim Kardashian are working really hard, so why not do what you love! Flow your passion and create your own ambition!

**Former Architect Creates Revolutionary Dating Site**
Lori Cheek is a NYC based architect who turned into an entrepreneur. Lori is the founder and CEO of Cheek'd, the reverse engineered dating site. Cheek'd allows people to give potential dates a physical card that entices the

potential date to interact with them in the virtual world. After its creation in 2010, Cheek'd has gone global with customers in 47 American states and 28 countries. Lori was listed in the Women 2.0's list of New York's Top Lady Led Startups and one of the top 10 CEOs to watch in 2013 on the American Express Open Forum. Cheek'd has received praise from numerous sources such as *The New York Times* which promptly told Match.com to move over and coined Cheek'd as the next generation of online dating. Not only did Cheek'd become successful and help many people, but it also allowed Lori to find a good companion. Lori met a man named Ray Bans at the beach, and she liked the way he looked. Lori decided to give him one of her own Cheek'd cards that said, "Let's meet for a drink." Not only did they meet for the drink, but now they hang out together. Lori Cheek's love for making online dating a little easier allowed her to find a good friend she never knew she had.

Now there is a Cheek'd app available on the Android and iPhone. This app allows people to buy cards that they can give to people nearby, and if you and the person you want to connect with both have the Cheek'd app, you can send a message to that person with the app. Cheek'd is revolutionizing online dating, and the only reason Cheek'd has gotten this far is because Lori loves what she does.

**How Getting Laid Off Changed Patricia's Life**
Patricia Nixon was 40 years old when she registered her business name, Nixon Virtual Strategies (NVS). NVS

provides virtual administrative assistant services to small and mid-sized businesses and entrepreneurs. The core services of NVS are WordPress website design, copywriting, blogging, and social media management. NVS is very flexible providing one-time and infrequent services for clients as well. Over the years, NVS has had many notable clients including the renowned Lisa McCourt who has sold over 5.5 million copies of her books. Patricia collaborated and assisted Lisa with her website design, book launches and tele seminars. Thomas Gagliano is another one of NVS's influential clients. Thomas is an author, life coach, and esteemed keynote speaker who is a frequent guest on television and radio broadcasts and often referred to in both printed and online publications. The list goes on and on, but another person Patricia has worked with is Jeffrey Fischer who was so impressed by their partnership that he wrote a blog post about how their work relationship began. Jeffrey has done several TEDTalks and is well known in his niche.

You can say that Patricia Nixon is now leading a good life. Patricia gets to help famous people, they write about her, and NVS continues to thrive. Before getting to this point, Patricia was earning what would appear to be a good salary but the costs to earn it were piling up. Prior to launching NVS, Patricia consulted at the NYC Mayor's Office as a Business Analyst earning $40 an hour and worked for well over 40 hours a week. However, there were several expenses involved that resulted in her having less money in the bank. Travel to and from work took over 3 hours every day from New York to New Jersey. Patricia would spend $14 for the round trip and another $4 daily for breakfast. In addition, she would regularly buy her own lunch, dinner, and there's also the dry cleaning costs. In the end, Patricia was easily spending $35 every day, and having to commute those 3 hours every day did not make anything better.

Then, Patricia got laid off from her consulting position. Losing the job made Patricia think of the things she loves to do but rarely made time for. One of those things happened to be writing. Although she did not know how writing would make her money, she started writing everywhere on the web.

With more time on her hands, Patricia was searching through career sites, and at the time, LinkedIn seemed to be the best choice for finding a career. Two weeks after Patricia created a LinkedIn account, that course of thinking changed. Patricia found out that discussions posted in LinkedIn groups tended to be one-way promotions in which no one would talk to anyone else. With that in mind, Patricia decided to write a lengthy post in the Forbes LinkedIn group. To her amazement, Carl Lavin, the Managing Editor of Forbes Magazine at the time, directly contacted Patricia asking if that blog post could be featured on the Forbes website. Patricia said yes and shortly after was invited by Carl to visit the Forbes offices and see what goes on behind the scenes in the newsrooms. Patricia got to tour the studio and meet Caroline Howard. Later, Lavin and Patricia had lunch and they talked about the power of words, and where they thought the digital world was heading. Being featured on Forbes' site allowed Patricia to get several interviews from radio stations and get to where she is today.

Although Patricia is living the good life with a prosperous business, she had a rough beginning. By staying true to her dreams and taking advantage of the free time adversity handed her, Patricia was able to rise above the difficulties of making money after being laid off. Not only does Patricia now make more money, but she does not have to endure the 3 hour commute on a daily basis. One thing Patricia learned from her experience is that you can earn a living without chasing assignments for the money alone. She focused on what she loved, ended up doing very well, and the money followed!

### How Danielle Russo-Slugh's Dedication To Help Her Husband Turned Into A Thriving Business

New Jersey native Danielle Russo-Slugh is an energized mother of two kids who thought she hit the jackpot when she became a trader on the floor of the New York Stock Exchange. After being on the floor of the NYSE for several years, life took a turn. That turn brought out the best leadership qualities in Danielle, and she is using those leadership qualities to grow a world class team of people. Danielle now has a successful business called Always

Energized which is a health, wellness, and life coaching business.

Danielle and her husband were both 9/11 volunteers, and a few years after that, her life changed forever. Her husband was diagnosed with stage 4 Hodgkin's Lymphoma which they both believe was related to the toxins they were exposed to at ground zero. After her husband got the diagnosis, Danielle decided to learn about detoxing the body and using super foods and nutrition to heal the body. In order to learn about detoxing the body, Danielle and her husband spoke with nutritionists and doctors, read books and online articles, and did as much research as they could to learn more about detoxing the body. Their efforts paid off and now Danielle's husband is in remission.

Not only did the diagnosis result in Danielle and her husband having a deeper appreciation for every day, but they were able to turn their newly acquired expertise about detoxing the body into a business. Danielle and her husband started sharing their expertise with people who wanted more energy, to lean out, to become better athletes, to age in a healthy manner, and to learn how to rid themselves of their cravings of coffee, soda, carbs, and sugar.

Danielle and her husband decided to close their business on the NYSE floor in December 2006 because they were getting outsourced by computers and algorithms. Although Danielle and her husband were outsourced from the NYSE floor, this closed door ended opening another door. In this case, that newly opened door led to health, happiness, financial freedom, and lifestyle choices. What started as a goal to save Danielle's husband from stage 4 Hodgkin's Lymphoma turned into the thriving business, Always Energized, with thousands of customers, many of whom have also decided to represent the company.

### Don Stewart Gave Up His Medical Career To Do What He Loves To Do

Don Stewart had a change in heart after completing his surgical internship. After accepting his hard-won medical license, he promptly discharged himself from the hospital. After discharging himself from the hospital, Don tried to identify a legitimate career path, and that legitimate career path became art. Don decided to go into the art niche because he had been doing art for his entire life without knowing. This kind of art was a way to get extra credit on homework assignments and a skinny kid's strategy for getting out of Physical Education class by adding an Art elective.

Over 150 humorous drawings and two books later, Don continues to love what he does and looks forward to coming back to the studio every day. Don gets out every now and then for art shows and book signings for his books, *DS Art--The Visual Humor of Don Stewart* and *Past Medical History--Recollections of a Medical Miscreant*.

By giving his interests a chance, Don ended up going from a job that he could not stand to doing what he loves every day. Don's art dream built momentum when a company of established graphic designers offered him a part-time job.

After that, Don's client list grew, he was able to pay the bills, and sure enough, Don was doing exactly what he loved.

Many people do not do what they love simply because they are afraid of losing their income and job in order to do what they love. Not only did Don sacrifice a lot of income by discharging himself from the hospital, but he also spent years in order to get to that level. Don was able to do what he loves after leaving a big-paying job. It is better to make a little less money and love what you do than it is to make a lot of money at a job that you dread everyday.

### Ed Doyle and RealFood Consulting--Delivering On Restaurant Visions

Ed Doyle is a passionate entrepreneur who founded RealFood Consulting, a restaurant advisory firm. Ed had a dream of creating his own restaurant, but he also realized that many restauranteurs dream of creating their own restaurants. As a result, Ed decided to combine his passion with helping others accomplish their dreams, and RealFood Consulting was born. Ed and his team at RealFood Consulting provide help--an intangible value. RealFood Consulting has allowed hundreds of people to accomplish their dreams of opening and successfully managing restaurants and concept spaces across the globe. RealFood Consulting provides independent restauranteurs with a certain level of resources and experience to help them start their own restaurants. Hiring other individuals like Ed and his team could cost $500,000 in salary, but as consultants who are able to step in at strategic points in the process, Ed and his team are able to considerably cut down the cost. Since RealFood Consulting started, it has grown its presence in multiple states and countries. Offices for RealFood Consulting are maintained in Boston, New York, and San Francisco with projects reaching as far as Kuwait. Before becoming an entrepreneur, Ed worked in the food service industry for the vast majority of his career, first as a chef and then as a culinary artist at restaurants in the Boston area. His team of consultants at RealFood Consulting have also worked in the food service industry for many years and have become experts of the industry. RealFood Consulting started because of Ed's passion for helping others accomplish their dream of starting and maintaining their own restaurant. Ed loves what he does, and he gets to experience the joy of helping others become successful while becoming successful in the process.

## How Kevin Hernandez's Love For Sports Turned Into The RecCheck App

Kevin Hernandez enjoys playing sports, and out of all of the sports, his favorite sport is basketball. Hernandez likes to play basketball since it is a competitive sport and it is easy to set up a game. However, a lot of times when Kevin wants to play a game of basketball, he ends up showing up to a completely empty basketball court. Kevin knew that this was a big problem, and instead of complaining about the problem, Kevin decided to create the solution.

Kevin's desire to solve a problem he had been experiencing for a long time resulted in RecCheck. RecCheck is a mobile app for organizing and discovering local pickup games. Users are able to set up a profile according to which sports they enjoy playing. Then, they can use RecCheck's maps to find or organize local games.

By building RecCheck, Kevin incorporated his love of sports into a business. When Kevin plays a pickup game with other people, he also gets to tell them about the app. Kevin does not see his business as "work" since he is still able to play pickup games. Actually, he is able to play more pickup games now since he no longer shows up to empty courts. Having his own business gives Kevin a lot of freedom such as the ability to exercise in the morning and play ball before he steps into the office. During an interview I had with Kevin, he said that he feels a lot more productive this way and can work on his own terms. To Kevin, his success is measured based upon how much he enjoys doing what he does.

By solving a problem he faced, Kevin was able to create his own business. You may be facing a problem and be looking for the solution. Instead of looking for the solution, it is entirely possible for you to create the solution and be the change that others are looking for...just like Kevin.

### Nicole Plummer Turns Her Love For Martial Arts And Fitness Into Her Own Business

Nicole Plummer knew right from the start that martial arts would become a big part of her life. She has been involved in coaching and fitness for 17 years, and she has practiced martial arts for over 20 years. Holding a 4th and 3rd degree black belts in two different martial arts styles, Nicole decided to take her love for martial arts all the way to the professional level where she won the North American Sports Karate Association and International Sport Karate Association World Titles. In addition, Nicole has been featured on ESPN 2 for the martial arts US Open. She has trained with many of the martial arts greats such as Master MaryBeth Klock-Perez, Grand Master Diego Perez, Sensei Robert Duzoglou, Mike Chaturanabut, Ming Lu, and fitness trainer Evelyn Rosenblatt.

In 2005, Nicole decided to start her own business with her martial arts and fitness skills. She trains individuals and groups in home, in facilities, and the outdoors and has been very successful at training all skill levels and ages. Some of the competitors Nicole has trained in sports martial arts competitions have won regional, state, and national titles in martial arts tournaments. A few of these champions include: Giselle S. (World Champion), Jassenia R. (National Champion), Marco C. (National Champion), Jordan F. (National Champion), and more.

Although Nicole was able to create a successful business based on her love for martial arts, she did not stop there. Nicole has been involved in a family-owned real estate business for several years. With the real estate business, Nicole is able to connect with her family, and they get to work together on managing and investing in real estate.

Even with two successful businesses, Nicole continues to grow. What started out as an idea to expand her own martial arts and fitness business turned into E Fitness Hub which is an online community website where individuals looking for services can find trusted health and fitness experts. In addition, health and fitness experts can use E Fitness Hub to network and build their businesses.

Nicole created three thriving businesses that all matched up with her passions. Instead of doing something for the sake of making money, Nicole pursued her passions. Pursuing her passions paid off. Nicole makes money by doing what she loves instead of making money just to survive.

## Graphic Designer Becomes Startup Founder

Jessica Greenwalt has been having so much fun designing and building businesses, that she forgot that it is work. Jessica has been a graphic designer for over 10 years and more recently, a startup founder. Jessica's design firm, Pixelkeet, works with companies from around the world to produce successful design projects. Her clients include LinkedIn, UC Berkeley, Marvel Comics, Telefónica, several Silicon Valley startups, and more.

Jessica is also one of the founders and lead designers for the med tech company, CrowdMed. CrowdMed uses the 'wisdom of the crowds' to solve difficult medical cases quickly online, and at a fraction of the cost compared to the traditional medical system. Before CrowdMed, this is how everyone would get the same answers: paying hundreds of thousands of dollars and visiting dozens of doctors over the span of several years.

Although Jessica gets stressed at times, she has a great team. Being at the CrowdMed office is like hanging out with college buddies while working on a fun and powerful project. Jessica and her teammates keep each other entertained as they help each other come up with solutions to tough issues, both in the company and in their personal lives. By working together throughout the years, Jessica and her team have become close friends, and to Jessica, her team is like family. Things that appear painful—such as staying up three days straight while on a business trip to launch a site before a conference—end up being fun for Jessica since she works with the right people. There is still some stress involved with her business, and Jessica finds moments of peace by maintaining a daily yoga routine, aiming for 7 hours of sleep every night, and reading during her morning commute on the BART.

It can easily be said the Jessica is a workaholic. Since Jessica loves what she does, she has never felt upset about working as much as she does. Although she sees work with a positive attitude, her friends and family have expressed concern about how much she works. Jessica thinks some workaholics are people who have found that their craft is the love of their life. The reason many people are puzzled by workaholism is because most of those people have not experienced doing what they love, which is exactly what Jessica is experiencing with Pixelkeet and CrowdMed.

## Dan Nainan's Journey To Becoming
## A World-Renowned Comedian

World renowned comedian Dan Nainan has not worked a single day in his life. Dan was fortunate enough to only get the jobs that he loved. His first job was senior engineer for Intel. At the time, Dan lived in Los Angeles, he read the newspaper often, but rarely read the job offers page. On one of the days that Dan happened to read the job offers, he saw Intel's job offer. The job's description said, "Tour the country for 2 months in 10 different cities for 2 years." As someone who loves to travel around the world, Dan saw Intel's offer as the perfect job.

Dan decided to call the number, but all he got was a FAX number. However, that would not stop Dan from getting his job. Dan ended up reversing the FAX number and directly called Intel. Dan knew that the person he called would either be very impressed or think Dan was creepy. Luckily for Dan, the person he called was very impressed that Dan found the number. This led to a job interview, and then Dan got hired for the job. Dan got to travel across the United States and traveled to European and Asian countries as well.

As the senior engineer for Intel, Dan had to speak on stage in front of thousands of people when he traveled to different cities. Although he loved seeing new places, he was afraid of speaking on stage and presenting demos. Since Dan knew he would have to speak on stage regardless of his fear, he knew that he needed to get more comfortable on stage. Dan took a comedy class where he had to perform on stage and get the audience to laugh in the same performance. Being a comedian and getting people to laugh while being on stage is more difficult than just being on stage. Since he did something more difficult, speaking on stage for Intel suddenly looked much easier. While talking with Dan, he compared this experience to baseball players. Some baseball players try to hit golf balls so it is easier for them to hit a baseball. That is exactly what Dan did for his Intel presentations when he took the comedy class.

Dan eventually became a natural on the stage. Word got out that Dan took comedy classes, and the people at Intel asked Dan to perform for them. Dan was initially scared of his first comedy performance, and he practiced his performance over and over again for weeks. When Dan did the performance, the audience loved him. Intel then asked Dan if he could perform again at the Intel dinner. After his performance went well at the Intel dinner, someone from Intel asked Dan to perform at the sales conference. For the comedy act at the sales conference, Dan imitated Intel's CEO in front of 2,500 people from all around the world.

At the end of the performance at the sales conference, people came up to Dan and said, "You're not an Intel employee. You're a professional comedian hired to pretend to be an Intel employee." As more people told him that he was a professional comedian, Dan realized that he could be a comedian for a living and pursue his dream. No matter how funny a comedian is, going from "just another comedian" to a world-renowned comedian is not an easy task. For doctors, lawyers, and many others, there is a template that explains what degrees these people need and what schools they have to go to in order to get the job. However, there is no template for a comedian. In the beginning, comedians are like leaves in a stream being buffeted around. They don't know the path, but by sticking with their profession, comedians gradually identify the path that they need to take. Comedians have to flounder around, look back at their performance, learn from their mistakes, and constantly improve. Dan had to do all of these things when he started out, and finding his path was not easy.

Just like many people, there was a point when Dan thought of quitting his job as a comedian. Dan got a club gig that did not go well. The audience did not receive Dan's jokes very well, and he went off stage after 5 minutes. All comedians, even the best comedians, bomb at a certain point. Although Dan really wanted to quit after that performance, he stuck with comedy.

After that performance, Dan decided to take comedy classes, and that's when everything started to fall in place. Dan's comedy teacher is a director from Stanford who knows a lot about comedy. Taking the class allowed Dan to learn more about comedy and become a better comedian. Dan still takes the class to this day. The same teacher helps Dan come up with some of his jokes.

After acquiring many skills in comedy, Dan asked a Robert Schimmel if he could perform at his show in Honolulu. Robert decided to give Dan a chance, and after the performance, Robert loved the performance. After that, Dan went on tours with Robert which allowed him to gradually go from "just another comedian" to a world-renowned comedian. After the tour with the producer, Dan learned that Russell Peters was doing some shows in NY. Russell gave Dan his phone number, and Dan decided to call Russell asking if he could be in any of Russell's performances. Instead of getting Dan on some of the shows, Russell told his agent to get Dan on every show. Dan got to travel across the United States again, and the many people in India started to notice. Touring with Russell sealed the deal, and now Dan was a world-renowned comedian. Since then, he has traveled to over 20 countries such as Singapore, India, Malaysia, Ireland, Turkey, England, Istanbul, Dubai, and others for comedy alone.

Dan was able to go from an unknown comedian to world renowned by aggressively asking for stuff, only doing clean comedy, identifying his target audience (Indian community), and marketing himself. Dan called many people telling them about what he does and if he could perform at the next event. These calls allowed Dan to perform at a lot of shows and become a very successful comedian.

After the interview, Dan shared some advice for all of the entrepreneurs and startups out there. While many people are in survival jobs (those 9 to 5 jobs), it is better to do something else that you love. If we work for 8 hours every day, then that is 33% of our lives. We better be doing something for 33% of our lives that we love to do.

In addition, time is our most valuable resource. When he was in college, Dan had a bad habit of playing too many video games and did poorly on exams. There are many people who say, "I do not have enough time," yet the average American watches 32 hours of television every week. You could do amazing things in those 32 hours. You can use that time to create products, learn how to code an app, and more.

Another important lesson is to ask people for stuff. There is nothing wrong with asking a question or asking if you can perform at someone's upcoming event. The worst thing that can happen is that the person denies you. Dan has asked numerous people if he could perform at other people's shows. Asking has allowed him to meet famous people such as Michael Bloomberg, Bill Clinton, Barack Obama, and others as well. Asking for what you want can lead to you getting what you want, just like it did for Dan.

# The Four Positions Of The Stampede

By utilizing the characteristics that create effective leaders (1) Good Planning, (2) Being An Innovator, (3) Time Management, (4) The Ability To Take Leaps, (5) Creativity, (6) Consistency, (7) The Ability To Know What Is Important, (8) Persistence, (9) The Ability To Make Connections, (10) Credibility, (11) The Desire To Become Successful, and (12) The Love For What You Do, you will be able to eventually lead your stampede. You will also need to identify where you currently are in your stampede, who the leaders of your stampede are, and how you can catch up to them. The four positions in the stampede are the leaders, the people in the middle, the people near the back, and the people who are far behind. In order to rank better in your stampede, you need to identify which of these four groups you fit in so you know where you need to go.

## The Leaders

Everyone wants to lead the stampede, but in a giant stampede, there can only be a few leaders. The leaders of the stampede are the ones with all of the characteristics of highly effective leaders. These leaders are the ones that we all talk about. They are well-known in many places. The name Larry Page should sound like a familiar one because his creation (Google) is in the front of its stampede.

## Who And What Leads The Stampede?

The people and businesses who are at the front of the stampede got there by combining all of the characteristics with a remarkable idea. Anything remarkable tends to start a stampede in which people try to be just as remarkable as the leader. The people leading the stampede for your niche are the people who are extraordinary. They may have a big following, a high quality product for a low price, or a training course with 4 hours of content more than the average training course. The remarkable people lead the stampede, and by being remarkable and utilizing the characteristics, you will be able to lead your niche's stampede too.

**The Middle Of The Stampede**
The middle of the stampede is filled with people who are close to the leader spot. You cannot necessarily think of the middle of the stampede similar to a hot dog bun with the hot dog in the middle. You must think of the middle of the stampede of people who are *really* close and capable of becoming the leaders of their stampedes. The only difference is that the leaders utilize a few of the characteristics slightly better than the people in the middle of the stampede.
In addition, the pioneers have a big advantage over the newcomers. MySpace was given a big advantage in the social networking world. They fouled it up. Facebook became next in line which is why it has more users than any other social network. It is possible for a newcomer to catch up with the pioneer, but the pioneer has a substantial advantage.

**Near The Back**
The people near the back of the stampede tend to have few characteristics of the leaders. These people lack the resources and knowledge to move themselves ahead. The people near the back are not nearly as well-known as the people in the front or middle of the stampede. However, this is not a permanent condition. If you do not know as much about your niche as the leaders do, you can read blog posts and books to learn more about your niche. Before I could write *How To Be Successful On Twitter*, I needed to learn how to effectively utilize Twitter. I started near the back, but by deciding to learn more about Twitter, I ended up writing a book about being successful on Twitter.

**Late Birds**
The people who get involved in a niche or innovation late are known as the late birds. Late birds do start out near the back. However, it is possible for these late birds to eventually lead their stampedes. Every author at one point was a late bird because there are millions of other authors. However, some authors were able to emerge as successful writers even though they were late birds.

**Why Do Leaders Fall Back?**
Some of the leaders do fall back. Some fall back because they are unable to innovate while others fall back because they stop taking leaps. Leaders have also lost their place in the stampede because of overconfidence, distractions, and

other reasons as well. Many of these leaders are remnants of what they once were.

## How Ranks Change

There are also reasons why some of the leaders fall back. In some cases, leaders fall so far behind that they become a memory of something that was once great. In this part of *Lead The Stampede*, you will learn about some of the people and businesses who are leading the stampede. You will also learn about the people and businesses who have lost their lead and become memories of the past.

## Case Study: MySpace

Remember when MySpace was the top social network? Just the thought of that sounds strange in a social networking world that is dominated by Facebook, Twitter, Google Plus, LinkedIn, Pinterest, and others as well. MySpace went from a famed social network to a remnant of something that was incredible. The reason MySpace collapsed is because the competition caught up. Mark Zuckerberg and Jack Dorsey decided to give the social network niche a try. Zuckerberg came up with Facebook while Dorsey came up with Twitter. Since then, more people are in the social network niche creating social networks that have impacted the world.

What happened to MySpace? Even with the advantage of being first, MySpace lost its place in the stampede. When MySpace was the first social network, the thought of MySpace being a powerhouse of innovation and change was not inconceivable. Then, Zuckerberg came and ended the short MySpace era. At this point, it could be argued that Facebook was just a really good competitor. MySpace wasn't forgotten about just yet. Then came all of the other social networks. Twitter, Pinterest, Instagram, Google+, LinkedIn, Snapchat, and all of the other social networks were created. As more thriving social networks made their way to the web, MySpace only became a memory. The reason MySpace is a memory is because its response to innovation was poor.

MySpace was the innovation, but then people made innovations to social media in general. All of the social networks are getting updates. Looking at Twitter's website back in 2006 shows how far the social network has gone. Many of the other social networks looked very similar. Facebook's website also looked bad when it first began. When many updates (the innovations), Facebook, Twitter, and the other social networks are what they are today. MySpace wasn't able to keep up with the changes that the other social networks were making. MySpace dropped all the way to the back of the stampede.

## Case Study: Pet Rock

Many people do not know about Pet Rock. The product was a rock, a nest, and a box. The idea of Pet Rock, a very creative one, turned a rock into a pet. Pet Rock ended up making over $1.5 million dollars in a year. Pet Rock was a profitable fad. Now, people wouldn't think of having a rock as a pet. Spending money to get a rock, a nest, and a box would be thought of as foolish. There are many rocks to pick up if someone really wanted to have a pet rock.

The problem is that Pet Rock wasn't consistent. The same Pet Rock was being sold again and again. People quickly realized that all they bought was a rock, a nest, and a box. The idea went from creative to boring. A rock can't interact like a dog or cat can. Since there was only 1 Pet Rock, return customers were unlikely. The only way for an author to have a returning customer is if the author has two or more books. Pet Rock never innovated their product, and as a result, people saw Pet Rock as what it really is: a rock, a nest, and a box.

**The Lack Of Innovation**

MySpace and Pet Rock fell to the back of their stampedes because they did not innovate. When innovative social networks were on the rise, MySpace could no longer keep up. MySpace went from new to old. All MySpace had to do was have more innovations. When Facebook launched, MySpace was still winning. If MySpace was as innovative as the other social networks, we would be talking about how *MySpace* was the first social network to reach 1 billion users instead of Facebook.

As strange as it sounds, Pet Rock was a booming business. It is entirely possible that Pet Rock would have survived for a longer period of time if it was innovative. Pet Rock could have made millions of more dollars by coming out with different pet rocks, drawing faces on the rocks, including a market so people could draw faces on their own rocks (that sounds strange too because you could do that with any marker or crayon, but the entire idea of Pet Rock sounds strange. If fast food restaurants that make people obese can stay in business, this sounds reasonable), including a certificate that could have said something like this, "I am the proud owner of my Pet Rock, _____." The thought of Pet Rock being a business to this day sounds strange. However, there were countless people who adored their Pet Rocks before the fad went away. If Pet Rock consistently made innovations and came out with new products, it would have carried on further. Pet Rock could have been around for another 5 years, 10 years, or even longer. There would have been more return customers as well. Who knows how much longer Pet Rock could have been in stores, and who knows how much more money Pet Rock could have made. In the end, Pet Rock fell to the back of their stampede just as quickly as it got to the front. These case studies show that in order to lead our stampedes, we need to be consistently innovative. When MySpace and Pet Rock got to the front of their stampedes, they forgot to consistently innovate. As a result, other competitors who consistently innovated were able to take advantage of MySpace and Pet Rock's faults. The competition honed in on MySpace and Pet Rock. When the competition honed in, MySpace and Pet Rock didn't stand a chance. Consistent innovators were able to claim the front of the stampede and dethrone those who stood in their way. If you are consistently innovative, you will be able to dethrone the leaders. Not only will you be able to dethrone the leaders, but you will also be able to stay in the lead once you get there.

## Keeping The Lead

Time and time again, leaders forget about keeping their lead. MySpace, Pet Rock, and many other businesses and people forgot about keeping their lead. There are upsets in sports because the underdog team wins plenty of games while the team that is expected to win loses plenty of games. The result is the underdog winning more games than the team that was expected to win and then advancing to the playoffs.

Once you move to the front of the stampede, it is important to keep your lead once you get there. Consistently being innovative is a start towards keeping your lead. By utilizing the characteristics of leaders, you will be able to lead the stampede and keep that lead. Getting the lead is a challenge, and once you get there, you don't want to lose it. Many people get overconfident when they become the leaders of the stampede. They get comfortable in their position but don't go through the uncomfortable schedules that got them where they are. Some of the leaders slow down in productivity because the thought of someone catching up is inconceivable. Before Facebook, who ever thought another social network would catch up to MySpace?

Competitors are always trying to catch up. They market and create products similar to the competition. When someone takes the lead, others try to catch up by following the pattern that person is using. Following the pattern will work for many people. Patterns are not difficult to follow. All you have to do to follow a pattern is find the directions and implement them. There are case studies in which competitors tell everyone about their strategy. This makes the how-to part easier to find. Since the directions are more accessible, more people can see them.

As more people see the directions, a surge of people implement the pattern. After the person with the $40 video game became successful, other video game producers decided to charge $40 for their video games as well. The first few people will succeed with this method, but most people will be the late birds who follow this method. A late bird can mean implementing the method months late. Being a late bird entirely depends on how quickly the pioneers respond. If the pioneers sell their video games for $40 within a a month, and then they become successful with the method, everyone else is a late bird. It is possible for a late bird to be successful, but it will be challenging.

**Late Bird Success Story: Pinterest**
Pinterest was launched years after Facebook and Twitter dominated the web. Even though all of Pinterest's other competitors were well established, Pinterest was able to become a successful social network. Pinterest reached 10 million unique monthly visitors faster than any other website. Now Pinterest is a powerful social network, and some statistics give Pinterest an edge on Facebook and Twitter. Pinterest came into the social media world later

than the other big players, but Pinterest was able to become a big player.

There are more social networks in existence than we realize, but many of them flop because those social networks are the late birds. Pinterest was able to succeed because it was different. Pinterest allows users to organize their posts differently from other social networks. By creating boards and putting posts on those boards, Pinterest allowed people to tell people about all of their interests and expertise while getting more followers. On Pinterest, it is possible to pin something about sports, famous people, and social media equally while being identified as a social media expert. On other social networks, posting about sports, famous people, and social media equally would rarely have that person identified as a social media expert.

Pinterest was ultimately able to succeed as a late bird because it was *different*. By being different, Pinterest satisfied the needs that social media users didn't even know they had: the need to categorize content based on hobbies, niches, sub-niches, products, and everything else.

### How David Carmell Started Late And Created A Business Based On His Past Needs

There are many established firms in the world, but there are also plenty of big names such as Goldman Sachs, Bloomberg, and Robin Hood Foundation. Creating a new firm and making that firm successful seems challenging in a competition with plenty of big names. However, David

Carmell was able to pull it off with his firm, C-Suite Advantage (www.csuiteadvantage.com). Carmell used to work as the president and majority owner of a transportation and logistics company. Carmell saw the need for C-Suite Advantage in his 50's when he saw a void and immediate need in the market.

The reasoning behind C-Suite Advantage is that Carmell felt that the advice being offered to the C-Suite was lacking. C-Suite Advantage is a firm that provides niche coaching and advisory services to business owners and CEOs. As the former CEO of a transportation and logistics company, Carmell wished that he could have had niche coaching and advisory services. In the end, he created a firm that would give what he wished for to other people. When Carmell advises clients, he gives them what they need to know...immediate gratification. Through insightful analysis, game changing advice, and understanding the client, Carmell is able to help leaders turn points of pain and problems of consequence into their strategic and financial advantage.

David Carmell saw a problem in the C-Suite and saw his firm as the solution. Even though there are many big name firms out there, Carmell still created his firm. Carmell was late to the party, but that did not stop him from implementing his idea. Now, C-Suite Advantage is a thriving firm that offers unique advice to CEOs and businesspeople.

### Nick Whitmore's Experience In The Thick Competition Of Freelance Writing

Nick Whitmore enjoys writing and was training to become a journalist. During the training, Nick thought it would make sense to become a freelance writer. By honing his writing skills and making money at the same time, it was a win-win situation for Nick. After being a freelance writer for a while, Nick decided to opt out of journalism. However, when there are millions of other freelance writers trying to get their slice of the pie, standing out as a freelance writer and making a strong income is not an easy task to accomplish. In addition, Nick started out making a small amount of money as a freelance writer which made it hard for him to pay the bills.

Nick was able to rise through the ranks and now has a plethora of clients. A big factor towards Nick's rise was his quality content. Clients enjoyed Nick's content so much that they told other people about Nick. Soon enough, Nick was getting client referrals left and right! With more offers coming in, Nick was able to raise his rates to something where he would be able to live a more comfortable lifestyle instead of barely making enough money to pay the bills. Even though Nick raised his rates, the offers keep on rolling in. Nick has written for several well-known websites such as CopyBlogger and ProBlogger. Although Nick decided to go into a very competitive niche, Nick was able to end up on top because of his persistence.

I was amazed by Nick's story and decided to ask him how he was able to remain persistent even when he was barely able to pay the bills. Nick said that by paying close attention to any job, you will become the best in your niche. If you continue producing quality content, you will get noticed. By getting noticed, you will be able to get referrals left and right. It is important to remember that Rome was not built in one day. It took much more than a day, but now Nick is easily able to pay the bills.

In order to stay persistent, you need to have a vision of your version of Rome. Nick's version was a full-time job as a freelance writer. Your version of Rome may be the bestselling book, the ability to work at home, or the $100,000 a year dream job that you love. It is important to strive for excellence in the beginning. Even when Nick was making $1 per article, he was striving for excellence. Because he strived for excellence from the very beginning, he now makes $1,000 for some of his articles. Don't wait for excellence to happen. You need to strive for excellence in order to become excellent.

### How Veronica Grey Went From A Few Google Search Results In 2009 To Numerous Search Results

Back in 2009, there were not a lot of Google results for Veronica Grey. There are many big name lifestyle experts such as Deepak Chopra, Marianne Williamson, and Eckhart Tolle who got to sit down on Oprah's couch that had numerous results show up on Google. Veronica decided to become a lifestyle expert even though she knew it would not be easy to become a big name like Deepak Chopra, Marianne Williamson, or Eckhart Tolle. Veronica was willing to try anything at that point because she had been trying to make a name for herself for over 15 years. Many failed attempts later, she simply thought, "Why not? I'll become a lifestyle expert."

Veronica got a lot of help from GuaranteedCelebrity.com which offers a step by step cookie cutter system to make a name for yourself no matter what you do. Veronica learned how to get in touch with TV stations who ended up inviting her on their shows. Veronica has made 45 appearances on TV in the past two years, and some of those appearances were on national shows such as "Good Morning America" and "Daytime."

Now, Veronica is a big name lifestyle expert. Now, you will be able to find a lot of Google results for Veronica. Although the chances of success were slim, Veronica was able to catch up to the big names and make 45 appearances on TV.

### Case Study: Maria Rekrut Gets Into Real Estate At 49 Years Old

Maria is now an individual who became wealthy when she became a real estate developer and investor who buys, holds and sells real estate. Maria's focuses on Bed & Breakfast and her successful Vacation Rental business. One of Maria's tips for people in real estate is to properly manage their real estate assets so that the real estates you buy are profitable. Maria started buying and selling real estate when she was 49, and with more than 10 years of experience, she has learned a lot about her niche. Maria was able to make the best of a late start. However, her journey to creating her real estate business was a rocky one.

Maria had gotten divorced several years before getting into the real estate business. Since Maria did not have a lot of money on her own, she had no other option but to work for minimum wage. After working for minimum wage for a few years, Maria decided that she had enough. She created her own Consulting Practice, Maria Rekrut & Associates in 1988 which was a business development, consulting, and seminar training company. Maria stopped her successful consulting practice in 2000 when she started to purchase real estate which led to her remarkable run of making millions of dollars by buying and selling real estate. Maria purchased a number of student rentals which turned into cash cows that allowed her to purchase more real estate. Maria also makes money by refinancing homes she owns and paid down debt or sold the properties which allows her to buy more real estate. Maria continues buying and selling real estate to this day.

**Who Said Retiring Was Mandatory?**
Art Koff worked for over 40 years in advertising and consulting, and in his late 60's, Koff retired from his job; however, Koff said that he needed another challenge in his life. Koff did not want to spend the rest of his life golfing, fishing, traveling, or doing anything similar without a challenge. While looking for a challenge, he decided to start a website to provide information to boomers, retirees, and

people planning their retirement. That website, RetiredBrains.com, was created in 2003. RetiredBrains.com also connects employers with older workers who are looking for employment.

Art Koff's message is to let other people know that retirement is not the end. Koff tells retirees that they can find a challenge in any area of expertise. As a result of the work he did researching content for his website, Koff became a powerful example of how older Americans can lead successful lives even after retirement. Koff has been interviewed on TV numerous times including a segment on *Fox News*. Koff is also a contributor for Market Watch which has an Alexa rank under 1,000.

Koff was brave enough to join a niche and take on a new challenge in his late 60's. Now, Koff is an inspiration for people who are planning their retirement. Koff was able to create a successful business in his 70's. He did join the niche late, but with hard work and dedication, he was able to become successful in his niche.

## The Newcomer To A Thick Competition

Imagine joining a niche where there are several companies making over $100 million. These big companies are able to hire employees and get more clients than startups. Alex Brola was up for the challenge. Alex went into the home cleaning niche because of the low barrier of entry. Alex was able to save a lot of money because people in the home cleaning niche do not need a brick and mortar business. Alex used a systematized process to ask people if they would like to take work from him as a contractor. For Alex, finding cleaners requires a systematized plan, not advertisements. While most cleaning companies continue using services such as Craigslist to promote themselves, Alex sticks with his systematized plan of getting more clients, and it works. Alex's business has numerous positive reviews on review sites such as Yelp, Yahoo Local, and Angie's Lists. Alex also uses these review sites to get new clients.

Alex was also able to take advantage of the relatively new Local SEO. An example of this would be searching for pizza stores nearby. The pizza stores with the best SEO appear on the top of Google's search results. Alex was able to take advantage of this feature and get more clients for his home cleaning business.

Alex's home cleaning company ended up making millions of dollars in revenue. This growth spurt came from Alex's marketing knowledge, and now all Alex must do is retain the revenue. Instead of waiting for investors or buying ads, Alex decided to use his knowledge to create a strong presence for himself in the home cleaning niche.

## Passionate Blogger Gets On ABC News And Yahoo! Finance

The Silicon Valley is the heartland for entrepreneurship, and I hope to visit some day. Many multimillion and multibillion dollars businesses such as Apple and Twitter started in the Silicon Valley. Many people in the Silicon Valley are either starting their own projects or companies, or they are working for a startup that they are really excited about. In the Silicon Valley, innovative ideas pop up all of the time. Shannon McNay jumped into the Silicon Valley tech scene in her 30's.

Before settling in the Silicon Valley, Shannon lived in New York and Ohio. Her two main motives to live in the Silicon Valley were to get paid as a writer and have a job in which she could make a serious impact. In the end, Shannon would be able to do both of those things. However, the start of her journey was a bumpy one.

Shannon had little experience with blogging when she started ReadyForZero as an intern. While interning, Shannon quickly learned the art of blogging, digital marketing, customer service, and the general tech space. Although she was learning more about blogging, digital marketing, customer service, and the general tech space, Shannon was still not getting a large amount of publicity for her efforts. Everything changed when Shannon learned about Credit.com. She learned about them through her social networks, and she shared a lot of their content with her followers, and soon enough, Shannon got her content on ABC News through a content partnership with Credit.com.

While she blogs, Shannon also helps people with their finances. Shannon generally helps her clients with optimizing their financial future by getting organized, finding ways to pay off debt faster, and improving clients' careers and relationships in relation to finances. Shannon empowers others through her education of finances.

# Conclusion

Leaders are influential individuals who pursue the ideas worth pursuing, make a positive change in the world, and have the proper mindset. They go the extra mile to get the job done and provide targeted people with something they would cherish. Leaders come from a variety of backgrounds, and the great thing is that anyone can become a leader. There are multiple leaders in a niche, and with the power of the internet, it is more possible than ever for people to go from the back of the stampede to the front of the stampede.

Every leader shares one thing in common. They all started from the bottom. Before the leaders led their stampedes, they were in the back and getting used to how their niches worked. The people in the back of your stampede who are currently unknown are following in the steps of Bill Gates, Steve Jobs, and all of the other iconic leaders of our time. Starting is one of the biggest steps that can be made, and it is starting that will allow you to get into the stampede. Few people even commit to get into the stampede, and many don't stay in the stampede for long. However, the stampede is something worth staying in so you move up, get more people listening, and then become the leader of your niche. When you become the leader of your niche, people will go to you for advice. They will ask you questions about your niche and buy your products that go into detail on certain aspects of your niche. Enjoy every second of your journey. Now, go forth, and lead your stampede!

## About The Author

Marc Guberti is a teenager entrepreneur, author, and digital marketing expert. Marc co-founded Teenager Entrepreneur, an online training course and in-person bootcamp dedicated to empowering others with the knowledge they need to become successful entrepreneurs. Marc has written multiple books such as *How To Be Successful On Twitter, How To Publish More Kindle eBooks Faster,* and *77 Powerful Methods To Get More Kindle eBook Sales.* You can find all of Marc's digital marketing articles on his blog at www.marcguberti.com.